THE CLASSICS OF
CATHOLIC SPIRITUALITY

The Classics of Catholic Spirituality

PETER JOHN CAMERON, OP

ST PAULS

Library of Congress Cataloging-in-Publication Data

Cameron, Peter John.
  The classics of Catholic spirituality / Peter John Cameron.
        p.   cm.
    ISBN 0-8189-0743-6
    1. Spirituality — Catholic Church.   I. Title.
    [DNLM: 1. Catholic Church — Doctrines.]
  BX2350.65.C36   1996
  248'.08'822 — dc20   95-50963
                                                  CIP

Produced and designed in the United States of America by the
Fathers and Brothers of the Society of St. Paul,
2187 Victory Boulevard, Staten Island, New York 10314,
as part of their communications apostolate.

ISBN 10: 0-8189-0743-6
ISBN 13: 978-0-8189-0743-2

Printing Information:

Current Printing - first digit   3 4 5 6 7 8 9 10

Year of Current Printing - first year shown

             2007 2008 2009 2010 2011 2012 2013 2014

For
my mother
and in memory of my father
with all my love

Permissions

The author wishes to thank the following publishers for their permission to reprint material from the following publications:

Excerpts from *Critical Theory Since Plato*, Revised Edition by Hazard Adams, copyright © 1992 by Harcourt Brace & Company, reprinted by permission of the publisher.

From *The Cloud of Unknowing and the Book of Privy Counseling* by William Johnston. Copyright © 1973 by William Johnston. Used by permission of Doubleday, a division of Bantam Doubleday Dell Publishing Group, Inc.

From *The Little Flowers of St. Francis* by St. Francis of Assisi. Copyright © 1958 by Beverly Brown. Used by Permission of Doubleday, a division of Bantam Doubleday Dell Publishing Group, Inc.

Reprinted from *Julian of Norwich* by Edmund Colledge, OSA and James Walsh, SJ, © 1978 The Missionary Society of St. Paul the Apostle in the State of New York and *Catherine of Siena* by Suzanne Noffke, OP © 1980 by same as above. Used by permission of Paulist Press.

Taken from *The Spiritual Exercises of Saint Ignatius*, translation and commentary by George E. Ganss, SJ, with permission of The Institute of Jesuit Sources, St. Louis, Missouri, copyright © 1992.

From *The Collected Works of St. John of the Cross* translated by Kieran Kavanaugh and Otilio Rodriguez © 1979, 1991, by Washington Province of Discalced Carmelites. ICS

Acknowledgments

I am deeply grateful to Mr. Fran X. Maier, the former Editor of the *National Catholic Register*, who offered me invaluable encouragement and guidance in my first writing endeavors. I am thankful as well to Mr. Joop Koopman the present Editor, and to Mr. Gabriel Meyer, the Associate Editor, who graciously invited me to write a series on the classics of Catholic spirituality for the *National Catholic Register*. Some of the following chapters appeared there first.

I would also like to thank all those who assisted me in any way in the writing of this book, especially Bishop Edwin F. O'Brien, the Rector of St. Joseph's Seminary (Dunwoodie), Professor Michael Gilligan, Fr.Gregory E.S. Malovetz, Jim and Diane Tomaszewski, Fr. Gregory Keeler, OP, Karen R. Castañeda for her secretarial assistance, Rev. Mr. John J. Higgins, who corrected the page proofs, Fr. Edmund C. Lane, SSP, the Editor, and Brother Aloysius Milella, SSP, the Editorial Coordinator of Alba House.

In a very special way, I would like to thank my beloved Dominican brother and friend, Fr. Romanus Cessario, OP, who was in every way the

Table of Contents

How to Read Classics of Catholic Spirituality

Time-Dated Material: Open Immediately. Who hasn't received so-marked items in the mail and promptly complied? And well we should. Any negligence on our part would render them worthless. But what about materials whose importance is not determined by time? Shouldn't we show them the same avid attention?

One of the richest treasures of Catholic tradition is its corpus of classic spiritual texts. What is a classic? Charles-Augustin Sainte-Beuve, a nineteenth-century French literary critic, defined it this way:

> A true classic is an author who has enriched the human mind, who has really augmented its treasures, who has made it take one more step forward, who has discovered some unequivocal moral truth, or has once more seized hold of some

eternal passion in that heart where all seemed known and explored; who has rendered his thought, his observation, or his discovery under no matter what form, but broad and large, refined, sensible, sane, and beautiful in itself; who has spoken to all in a style of his own which yet belongs to all the world, in a style which is new without neologisms, new and ancient, easily contemporaneous with every age ("What is a Classic?" in *Critical Theory Since Plato*, Hazard Adams, ed. San Diego: Harcourt Brace Jovanovich, 1971, 555-562. This citation: p. 557).

From this definition we can glean the purpose of the classic, namely, to increase the store of human knowledge, especially by highlighting moral truths; to improve what we know by enriching and advancing human thought; and in the process to rekindle dormant feelings about the truths we value. This goal is particularly apropos to Catholic spiritual classics.

True classics are those that have stood the test of time by transcending cultural peculiarities and overly-specific interests. Their relevance reaches beyond the author's day and age so as to speak cogently to the questions and concerns of people of every era. As Sainte-Beuve writes:

The idea of a classic implies in itself something which has sequence and solidity, which forms a whole and makes a tradition, something which has 'composition,' is handed on to posterity and lasts (*ibid.*, 556).

What the classics say is valuable to all, and the way they say it makes them available to all. A true classic is both enduring and endearing.

The classics present us with a challenge to look beyond our limited personal experiences and prescribed social standards. They entreat us to put our trust in the purview of those who have gone before us, despite the distance of history. They prompt us to risk relying on the authority, admiration, and wisdom of those unfamiliar with our modern anxieties.

However, in order to benefit from the riches of the classics, it is good to keep a few basic guidelines in mind. First of all, in reading a Catholic classic we must remind ourselves why it was written. Invariably a book is authored with a specific purpose in mind. It intends to achieve some particular aim. Therefore, in taking up a classic, one of the first things we should do is to identify the author's objective. This is accomplished by examining the background and circumstances of the book.

We come to a better understanding of the purpose of a classic once we have noted the nature of the text. For example, is the book apologetic in nature? That is, does it set out to defend the truths of the faith? Or is it more evangelical in focus

— designed to stir our hearts to belief? Perhaps the work is chiefly catechetical, ordered to deepening the reader's grasp of particular doctrinal teachings. Therefore, in reading a classic we must appropriate what it is the author wants to accomplish. That saves us from the temptation of imposing our own designs on a text — from reading into it.

Secondly, we must acknowledge for whom the book was written. Who was the author's audience? Why was the book important to them? What was going on in their lives? By trying to unite ourselves with the experiences of that target audience we can authentically appreciate both the strong points and the limitations of the text, for we are not the people the author had in mind. Sometimes we tend to forget that and grow frustrated when the author's writing fails to speak more directly to our current needs. However, it is unfair to attempt to read a classic strictly from our point of view. Instead, our responsibility in reading a classic is to extrapolate its still-pertinent meaning and apply it to our lives.

And thirdly, we must consider the cultural factors that color a given work. It is not uncommon to be put off by an older book because of its foreign sounding literary style. Nevertheless, in order to enter into the world of a classic we are asked to adopt a forgiving disposition that enables us to look beyond literary limitations, awkward expressions, and obsolete ideas. To profit from a classic we must take the good with the bad. The energy this requires of us is worth all our effort, for as Sainte-Beuve reminds us:

> There comes a period in life when, our wanderings all finished and our experiences all acquired, there is no keener pleasure than to study and deepen the things we know, to relish what we taste, just as when you behold again and again the people you love; purest delight of the mature mind and taste. It is then that this word classic assumes its true meaning (*ibid.*, 562).

Unfortunately, the particular spiritual pleasure proffered by the Catholic classics is not self-evident to all. Therefore, the specific aim of this book is to provide a theological reflection on and practical guide to a number of great Catholic texts. It seeks to demonstrate the critical relevance of the classics of Catholic spirituality to contemporary faith-living. In short, the book is meant to persuade us to grow in our esteem of the voices that went before us so as to deepen the faith that we profess with our own voice.

Sometimes past insight sheds the best light on present perplexity. It is a truly Catholic act, then, to rely on the model of holiness revealed to us by the Church's outstanding spiritual writers. For from the classic authors, "these good and ancient spirits" who "give us back our own thoughts in full richness and maturity" we gain "an unwavering friendship which will never fail us, and that habitual impression of serenity and sweetness, which reconciles us, who so often need it, to mankind and to ourselves" (*ibid.*, 562).

The wisdom of the Catholic classics moves us to pull those neglected volumes from the shelf, to blow off the layers of dust, and to read between the lines: *Timeless Material: Open Immediately.*

1

Confessions

In an age of unfettered secularism and religious antipathy being a Catholic can seem downright absurd. Where might the contemporary Catholic turn to find a role model… guidance… empathy with so many daily struggles?

Every day the ordinary Catholic confronts a host of trying and controversial issues. They range from wrestling with fundamentalism, to coping with addictive and emotionally abusive personalities (especially within the family), to counteracting society's obsession with sex, to contending with ambivalence and inertia regarding meaningful commitments. Where can we go to find a compelling story that speaks to the sum of these our experiences? The answer is the *Confessions* of St. Augustine, for — in his own life in the fourth century — St. Augustine personally dealt with each of these dilemmas.

What does the title of his book signify? When we hear the word "confessions" we're inclined to think of those innumerable tell-all talk shows that blister the airwaves with exhibitionistic revelations. However, St. Augustine's use of the term refers to something altogether different.

St. Augustine intended his *Confessions* to be a sacrifice of love offered to God: "I will now call to mind my past foulness and the abominable things I did in those days.... not because I love those sins, but so that I may love you....The memory is bitter, but by it you grow sweet unto me.... I write this book for love of your love."

In so doing, St. Augustine hopes to prompt others to join him in his praise of God's mercies: "I shall tell how it was that you broke the chains that bound me; and all who worship you, when they hear this, will exclaim, 'Blessed be the Lord in heaven and on earth.'" At the same time, St. Augustine realizes that such a recounting will fire the hearts of his readers with the love of God. This in turn should inspire them to offer their own confessions to God: "It is by confessing our own miserable state and acknowledging your mercy towards us that we open our hearts to you, so that you may free us wholly.... Then we shall no longer be wretched in ourselves, but will find our true happiness in you."

Confessions thereby profoundly demonstrates the importance of possessing a healthy sense of sin. One of the main reasons people shirk sacramental confession is because they consider it redundant to tell God sins he already knows. However, as St. Augustine points out: "A person who confesses to you does not teach you what takes place within him as though you did not know it." Rather, as St. Augustine's testimony asserts, confession of sin sanctifies us in three ways. It saves us from the misery of having to deal with our failings alone. It provides the first essential step in loving God. And it causes us to deepen our delight in God's mercy as we retain a contrite memory of our sins.

St. Augustine's invitation to share in the grace of such confession especially entices us because it comes from a person utterly like ourselves. Augustine's original repugnance of Christianity stemmed from a fundamentalist reading of the Scriptures. "Certain Old Testament passages had been death to me when I took them literally." The preaching and spiritual direction of St. Ambrose inspired in Augustine an abiding love for the Word of God. His experience helps enlighten Catholics besieged by those critics given to reading the Bible over-literally.

St. Augustine was no stranger to family dysfunction. For a period of time as a young woman, Augustine's mother Monica struggled with alcohol. The saint recalls: "My mother used to tell me herself that there had crept upon her a secret love of wine." Once Monica confronted the fact of her addiction, she was blessed with a cure from God.

Patricius, the father of Augustine, struggled

with emotional abuse. *Confessions* relates his marital infidelity and his "hot temper." In the last days of his life, Monica managed to convert her husband... the foreshadowing of the conversion of her son.

Augustine's own ensnarement in sensuality is legendary... a vice that conflicted Augustine first with the life and then with the death of a son born out of wedlock. His ambivalence to commit himself to the Truth is an all too relevant theme. "Give me chastity and continence, only not yet." It was not until Augustine glimpsed the beauty of Continence, imaged as a beautiful woman, "a fruitful mother of children," that Augustine found the strength to give himself completely to God. That vision served as the catalyst of his conversion. And thus he could confidently proclaim: "Even though a soul clings to things of beauty, if their beauty is outside God, the soul is riveted only upon sorrow."

Despite its occasional references to vanished heresies and removed philosophical arguments, *Confessions* remains required reading for any Catholic serious about the faith. Its crucial lesson about how to recognize sin and deal with it is better taught nowhere else. As a bonus, *Confessions* provides invaluable insight about the power of intercessory prayer and how to understand petitions that seem to go unanswered. In addition, St. Augustine's own words help dispel the myth of alleged sexism, as when he attests that, "in her mind and her reasonable understanding, woman has a nature the equal of man's."

Why else read *Confessions*? Because it reveals the catholicity of irksome issues that to this day continue to challenge us. In so doing, it provides solace, wisdom, counsel. But perhaps the single best reason for reading *Confessions* is to engage the personality of a truly great saint and Father of the Church who comes to us, not as a venerable hierarch, but as a vulnerable sinner, speaking with candor, humility, and healthy shame. His words beckon us to believe: "If this happened to me, just think what God's grace can do for you!"

2

The Cloud of Unknowing

The unknown English author of the fourteenth century work *The Cloud of Unknowing* begins his book with a word of caution for the spiritually fickle: "You are not to read it... unless you [are] a person deeply committed to follow Christ perfectly. I have in mind a person who, over and above the good works of the active life, has resolved to follow Christ... into the inmost depths of contemplation." The author aims to weed out "worldly gossips, flatterers and fault-finders, talebearers and busybodies, or the plainly curious — educated or not."

The book is intended for those not content with a mundane Christian existence. And this is rather daunting. For the contemplative life requires a serious commitment not compatible with many of our common comforts. The author prescribes two prerequisites for contemplative prayer: "If you ask who should take up contemplation I would reply: all those who have sincerely forsaken the world and who have set aside the concerns of the active life.... If you ask me when a person should begin the contemplative work I would answer: not until he has first purified his conscience of all particular sins in the sacrament of penance."

It is not an anti-intellectual bias but rather a theological truth that restricts the merely curious from this endeavor. "Thought cannot comprehend God," *The Cloud* contends. "And so, I prefer to abandon all I can know, choosing rather to love him whom I cannot know. Though we cannot know him we can love him. By love he may be touched and embraced, never by thought."

However, more than just the natural limitations of the human mind move the author away from a conceptual kind of prayer. He realizes that our very thoughts and ideas must themselves be purified by Jesus in order to become worthy instruments of worship. "Natural intelligence is turned to evil whenever it is filled with pride and unnecessary curiosity about worldly affairs and human vanities, or when it selfishly covets worldly dignities, riches, empty pleasures, or flattery."

The Cloud then calls for a rigorous reordering of the priorities of the modern mind prone to equate knowledge with power. In this way, love assumes its rightful primacy in the life of prayer. The author teaches that "it is far better to let your mind rest in the awareness of God in his naked existence and to love and praise him for what he is in himself."

To pray in this way, we must be willing to give ourselves to God through acts of love and not through cogitation. In terms of motivation, we must love God for himself, and not because of what he does for us. "This is what you are to do: lift your heart up to the Lord, with a gentle stirring of love, desiring him for his own sake and not for his gifts.... In the contemplative work God is loved above every creature purely and simply for his own sake. Indeed, the very heart of this work is nothing else but a naked intent toward God for his own sake."

Having outlined the theological principles for contemplation, the author next supplies practical instructions for carrying it out. Here we learn the doctrine of the two "clouds."

First of all, what are we to do with the memory of our past sins, with the temptation to new sins, with the clever and even holy thoughts that plague us as we attempt to give ourselves undividedly to God? "You must fashion a cloud of forgetting beneath you, between you and every created thing.... You are to concern yourself with no creature whether material or spiritual nor with their situation and doings whether good or ill."

How many of us have felt our prayer life falter because of the innumerable distractions that constantly besiege us? The author of the *The Cloud* understands this dilemma: "When you most desire to be alone with God, distracting concepts will slip into your mind with such stealth that only constant vigilance will detect them. Be sure that if you are occupied with something less than God, you place it above you for the time being and create a barrier between yourself and God."

Unfortunately, many Christians try to conquer their distractions by actively engaging them. *The Cloud* recommends a better strategy: "Say to your thoughts, 'You are powerless to grasp God. Be still.' Dispel them by turning to Jesus with loving desire.... If you pay attention to these ideas they will have gained what they wanted of you, and will go on chattering until they divert you even more.... Before you know it, your mind is completely scattered." Therefore, the author encourages: "You must abandon them all beneath the cloud of forgetting.... Crush them beneath your feet and bravely step beyond them."

Once we have left these things behind, just where exactly do we step to? To the cloud of unknowing. The cloud of unknowing is that spiritual state "where in secret and alone the believer centers all his love on God." It is a place where "one turns to God with a burning desire for himself alone and rests in the blind awareness of his naked being." It is called the cloud of unknowing because "in the beginning it is usual to feel nothing but a kind of darkness about your mind or, as it were, a cloud of unknowing. You will seem to know nothing and to feel nothing except a naked intent toward God in the depths of your being.... It is a darkness of unknowing that lies between you and your God."

In order to facilitate that turning to heaven, *The Cloud* exhorts us to adopt a short prayer-word that enables us to focus our love steadily on God. "Gather all your desire into one simple word that the mind can easily retain.... This word will be your defense in conflict and in peace. Use it to beat upon the cloud of darkness above you and to subdue all distractions, consigning them to the cloud of forgetting beneath you."

Such unmitigated love on our part will not go unrewarded. *The Cloud* describes several reciprocal benefits. "The contemplative work of love by itself will eventually heal you of all the roots of sin." Moreover, it advances our growth in divine intimacy and liberates us from the urgings of temptation: "As your heart grows in purity of spirit, it is less dominated by the flesh and more intimately united to God."

At the same time, "the work of love nurtures practical goodness." "The warmth [of the con-templative's] love reaches out to all, friend, enemy, stranger, and kin alike." The author notes that the contemplative's "whole personality becomes so attractive that good people are honored and delighted to be in his company, strengthened by the sense of God he radiates." And finally, even homeliness gets a help in contemplation: "It seems to transfigure a person even physically so that though he may be ill-favored by nature, he now appears changed and lovely to behold."

The final word regarding *The Cloud of Unknowing* is the author's own: "The more often you read it the better, for that much more shall you grasp of its meaning."

3

The Little Flowers of St. Francis

"This book contains certain little flowers, miracles, and inspiring stories of the glorious little poor man of Christ, Saint Francis, and of some of his holy companions," declares the frontispiece of *The Little Flowers of St. Francis*. The work was written by an Italian Franciscan, Brother Ugolino di Monte Santa Maria, around 1330 — a hundred years after the saint died. As such, this little book celebrates the spiritual legacy of the Franciscan Order.

It begins by narrating appealing stories about St. Francis of Assisi that — apart from any properly historical purpose — manifest how he personally embodied the charism of the Order he founded. Early on, the book relates St. Francis' famous sermon to the birds, which illuminates the saint's theology of sanctity: "My little bird sisters, you owe much to God your Creator, and you must always and everywhere praise him because he has given you freedom to fly anywhere. So the Creator loves you very much, since he gives you so many good things." St. Francis esteems the bird's privilege of flight as a true fruit of the poverty so essential to the Franciscan conception of holiness. It was blessed poverty "who accompanied Christ on the cross, was buried with Christ in the tomb, and with Christ was raised and ascended into heaven, for even in this life she gives to souls who love her the ability to fly to heaven, and she alone guards the armor of true humility and charity."

A different animal serves to amplify another important aspect of Franciscan spirituality. The savage wolf of Gubbio threatened to devour every living thing in the village, so "rabid with hunger" was it. In a sense, the wolf represents the fierceness of untamed human nature and how we would act left to ourselves outside of grace. But the grace-filled Francis was not afraid to go "where the wolf lives." At the moment the beast threatened to attack him, Francis made the sign of the cross, at which "the wolf closed its terrible jaws and stopped running; it lowered its head and lay down at the saint's feet, as though it had become a lamb."

This "conversion" effected by the power of the cross is completed in a pledge. Francis says: "Brother Wolf, I promise you that I will have the people of this town give you food every day as long as you live, so that you will never again suffer from hunger." As the author relates: "The wolf lived two years more, and it went from door to door for food. It hurt no one, and no one hurt it.

The people fed it courteously. And it is a striking fact that not a single dog ever barked at it. Then the wolf grew old and died. And the people were sorry, because whenever it went through the town, its peaceful kindness and patience reminded them of the virtues and the holiness of St. Francis." What was once feared for its ferocity had become an intimate object of fondness. Such is the transformative power of grace: "If the Lord should make stones and rocks rain from heaven, they would not hurt us if we were what we should be. If a man were what he should be, evil would be changed into good for him."

St. Francis' ability to subdue was not limited only to the onslaught of wild beasts. He was equally effective with assaults from his own kind. Once when Francis was preaching to the Saracens, a certain woman who was "very beautiful in face and body but very foul in mind and soul" solicited the saint. In reply to her seductive proposition, St. Francis said: "If you wish me to do what you want, you must also do what I want." With that, the saint "stripped himself naked and threw himself down on the fire in the fireplace as on a bed. And he called to her: 'Undress and come quickly and enjoy this wonderful bed, because you must be here if you wish to obey me!'" The shock of the miraculous invitation caused a profound repentance in the woman that led her later on to become an instrument of conversion for many others.

Where did St. Francis derive the strength and confidence to confront victoriously the evil forces of nature? From his personal sharing in the Passion of Christ. In his body, St. Francis bore the sacred wounds of the Lord's crucifixion — the Stigmata. Jesus himself reveals to Francis the purpose of this grace: "I have given you the Stigmata which are the emblems of my Passion, so that you may be my standard-bearer." And although he tried hard to hide the wounds from the sight of others, those he encountered could not help but to recognize the divine power flowing from them.

The mortification St. Francis experienced in his body helped him to see the importance of subordinating the flesh to the spirit. By means of this insight Francis gained great mastery over temptation. When Brother Leo was besieged by spiritual temptations, St. Francis confided: "I love you more, the more you are attacked by temptations. Truly I tell you that no one should consider himself a perfect friend of God until he has passed through many temptations and tribulations." For "the more grace a man has, the more the devil attacks him."

We should not be surprised at the manner of the evil one's attacks, for when "the devils cannot harm and trouble holy and perfect men by terror, they turn to another method and temptation: pride and vanity." In this regard, Brother Giles warns: "I find many people who work for their body and few who work for their soul.... Our flesh is like a hog that runs eagerly into the mud and enjoys being in the mud.... It is impossible for a man to attain to grace unless he gives up sensuality.... Unless a man prepares a place for God within himself, he will never find a place among the creatures of God." To this end, even the slightest transgression must be avoided, for "through a small sin, a man may lose a great advantage for his soul."

The key, then, for dealing with temptations is a rectified self-knowledge that keeps us mindful of our faults. "He who always keeps his sins before his eyes will not weaken in any tribulation.... Blessed is he who always has his sin and the goodness of God before his eyes and who patiently bears all tribulations and trouble, for he can look forward to a great consolation."

At the same time, a humble self-regard must always be tempered by the truth of God's mercy. "You must always believe that God's power to forgive is greater than your power to sin." *Little Flowers* recounts the story of an ailing friar who allowed himself to become blackmailed by sin: "But what was worse than all the other afflictions was that a devil stood before him holding a large scroll on which were written all his sins and faults and failings of thought and deed, and the devil said to him: 'Because of all these things which you thought and said and did, you are damned to the depths of hell!' And the sick friar forgot all the good things that he had ever done, and that he was or ever had been in the Order."

This story illustrates how much authentic self-knowledge relies on informed confidence in God's mercy. Without it, we become forgetful and doubtful not only of our good works, but of our very calling from God. Brother Matthew comes to the sick friar's rescue: "Don't you remember that the mercy of God is greater than all the sins in the world, and that Christ Our Blessed Savior paid an infinite price to God our Father in order to redeem us?" His reminder is meant also to heal and uplift us when we become beset by despair. "No sinner should ever despair of God's mercy as long as he lives. For there is hardly a tree so thorny and knotted that men cannot make it smooth and beautiful. So likewise there is no sinner in this world so bad that God cannot adorn him in many ways with grace and virtues."

However, we should not become discouraged if our growth in grace takes time or occurs obscurely. As is the case with one friar, "it pleased God in his goodness to withdraw that light and fire of divine love from him and to deprive him of all spiritual consolations, leaving him without love or light and utterly miserable and depressed and mournful." God's loving Providence and purpose are fully at work in moments of such aridity, for "the longing of holy men increases to greater love and merit when God delays in granting its fulfillment."

In the grip of aridity, Franciscan poverty impels us to surrender our anxieties and ambitions to God in the certain hope that he will provide everything we need to be holy and happy. For this reason, "St. Francis did not like the ants very much because they were too anxious about collecting their food, but he liked the birds more because they do not gather into barns." St. Francis himself learned this lesson poignantly through the experience of the Stigmata which "gave unbearable pain to his flesh and physical senses," diminishing his physical strength so that he was no longer able to have charge of governing the Order.

In the end, the somewhat forward words of a simple peasant to St. Francis engage everyone committed to the Franciscan way of holiness: "Try to be as good as everyone thinks you are, because many people have great faith in you. So I urge you: never let there be anything in you different from what they expect of you."

4

Revelations of Divine Love

Julian of Norwich was a fourteenth century an-chorite attached to the church of St. Julian in Norwich, England who described herself as "a simple, unlettered creature." Yet, in her reclusive contemplation Julian received spiritual revelations from the Lord which she recounted in 1373 in her book entitled *Revelations of Divine Love*.

In presenting her account, Julian hoped to provide "many words of comfort for all those who desire to be Christ's lovers." She further specifies her audience when she prays that the book might be read only by "those who will submit themselves to the faith of Holy Church."

The hallmark of Julian's insight is her insistence that Christians both take delight in God and realize how much delight they give to God. Julian writes: "It is God's will that we have true delight with him in our salvation. For we are his bliss, because he endlessly delights in us." In another place, she spells this out: "We are Jesus'. We are the Son's crown, which crown is the Father's joy, the Son's honor, his reward, the Holy Spirit's delight, and endless bliss." Julian instructs that Jesus wants us to pay heed to this bliss for the sake of our salvation, while we at the same time share equally in the delight of God. As she puts it: "Our Lord wants us to be occupied in this: rejoicing in him, for he rejoices in us."

But how exactly do we give delight to God? What does it entail? It begins by recognizing the truth that God "made us only for himself." The *Catechism of the Catholic Church* reinforces this understanding when it states: "Man is created by God and for God.... Man alone is called to share, by knowledge and love, in God's own life. It was for this end that he was created, and this is the fundamental reason for his dignity." (27, 356)

The dynamic of giving God delight has several aspects. As Julian explains, it first of all means devoting ourselves to a life-long search for the divine: "It is God's will that we seek on until we see him, for it is through this that he will show himself to us.... The soul's constant search pleases God greatly.... God wishes to be known, and it pleases him that we should rest in him." The *Catechism* puts it this way: "The desire for God is written in the human heart.... God never ceases to draw man to himself. Only in God will he find the truth and happiness he never stops searching for." (27) We delight God, therefore, when we carry on this initiative that he implants in our hearts.

In the process, we discover and fulfill our God-given vocation: "The human person is from his very conception ordered to God and destined for eternal beatitude.... The Beatitudes respond to the natural desire for happiness. This desire is of divine origin: God has placed it in the human heart in order to draw man to the One who alone can fulfill it.... The Beatitudes reveal the goal of human existence, the ultimate end of human acts: God calls us to his own beatitude." (1711, 1718, 1719) Julian of Norwich expresses her grasp of this: "We long to be filled with endless joy and bliss, for we are made for this."

Therefore, in order to see God in the way that he wills to show himself to us, we must first be willing to see and know ourselves in truth. Julian writes: "We can never come to the full knowledge of God until we first clearly know our own soul. For until the time that it is in its full powers, we cannot be all holy.... Our passing life that we have here does not know in our senses what our self is, but we know in our faith." The ability to delight God, then, requires that we look for self-worth and meaning — not in the world or through our senses, but — in our faith. "When we know and see, truly and clearly, what our self is, then we shall truly and clearly see and know our Lord in the fulness of joy." A grace-filled grasp of self fills us with a bliss that in turn gives delight to God.

On a practical note, Julian makes a connection between sanctity and risibility. In fulfilling our duty to give delight to God, the anchorite urges us to make use of one distinctly human, but often undervalued, property: our sense of humor. "It is pleasing to Christ that we laugh to comfort ourselves, and that we rejoice in God because the devil is overcome." Such laughter is a personal confirmation of the right kind of trust and conviction we are called to embrace. Julian reassures us that "the greatest honor which a soul can pay to God is simply to surrender itself to him with true confidence." And holy laughter is one helpful way.

From where do we derive the privilege of delighting in God and of returning that delight to him? Julian tells us: "By the power of the same precious union by which God joined us to himself we love our Creator and delight in him, praise him and thank him and endlessly rejoice in him." Union with God, then, signals the deepest longing of the divine will. "Our courteous Lord wants us to be as familiar with him as heart may think or soul may desire." In fact, Julian goes so far as to encourage us to assume that all of God's great works have been accomplished for us personally as a sign of his love: "It is God's will that I see myself as much bound to him in love as if everything which he has done he had done for me."

If we are stunned by such boldness, we must

remember that Julian herself felt this way first: "I was greatly astonished that he who is so to be revered and feared would be so familiar with a sinful creature living in this wretched flesh." No wonder it remains impossible to have perfect rest or true happiness until we are "substantially united" to God. He invites us to such familiarity so that he might "delight to reign blessedly in our understanding, and sit restfully in our soul, and dwell endlessly in our soul, working us all into him." The authentic fulfillment of our soul depends on our free and complete response to this divine offer, for "our soul may never have rest in anything which is beneath itself."

If we experience certain unease in our life, we can attribute it to our failure to regard "as nothing all things which are created." For only when the soul "has become nothing for love, to have him who is everything, is it able to receive spiritual rest." Therefore, "God wishes to be known" in order to undo the misconceptions we have about him and about creation. And even though "no created being can know how much and how sweetly and how tenderly the Creator loves us," we nevertheless "persevere in spiritual contemplation" in order to benefit from the graces of that mysterious relationship.

We should not recoil if fear accompanies our growth in God. As Julian instructs us, "love and fear are brothers, and they are rooted in us by the goodness of our Creator." The loving contemplation of God fills us with reverent fear and true meekness, a rectified humility, and a recharged love for our neighbors. "When we have a strong and wise love for Jesus, we are at peace." The union that God draws us to here on earth directs us to our ultimate union with the saints in heaven. Julian assures us that even "before God made us he loved us," which convinces us that "we are made for love, in which love God endlessly protects us." At conception, the soul is "preciously knitted to God"; in heaven, all the saved souls "are knit in this knot, and united in this union." The intensity of divine love never varies, for God "loves us now while we are here as well as he will when we are there, before his blessed face." However, God does "make the soul's service known to all who are in heaven" so that the sanctified might become "endless marvelous bliss to all who are in heaven."

It may be difficult for us to accept this teaching, especially when faced with the agony of sin or suffering. And yet, Julian insists: "We need to fall, and we need to see it; for if we did not fall, we should not know how feeble and how wretched we are in ourselves, nor, too, should we know so completely the wonderful love of our Creator." When in her prayer Julian asked Jesus "why sin was not prevented," the Lord answered her with the words, "Sin is necessary." For, as Julian came to understand, "every man needs to fail and to be left to himself. God wishes us to know that he keeps us safe all the time, in joy and in sorrow, and that he loves us as much in sorrow as in joy." Only the painful experience of personal sin "purges us and makes us know ourselves and ask for mercy."

But we must be vigilant not to give into the deceptions of the devil. "It is the enemy who wants to retard us with his false suggestions of fear about our wretchedness. For it is his purpose to make us so depressed and so sad in this matter that we should forget the blessed contemplation of our everlasting friend." However, despite the horror of our sin, the truth is that God "will not reveal it to us except by the light of his mercy.... God in his courtesy measures the sight of our sin for us; for it is so foul and so horrible that we should not endure to see it as it is."

The only holy response to such a vision is to "acknowledge our wretchedness and flee to our Lord," for "the more abased we are, the more profitable it is for us to touch him.... He wants us promptly to attend to the touching of his grace, rejoicing more in his unbroken love than sorrowing over our frequent failings." We discover the right standard for measuring the gravity of our sinfulness in remembering that "the Lord takes the falling of any creature who will be saved no harder than he took the falling of Adam." Therefore, in the face of sin we are called to "contemplate the Lord's glorious atonement, for this atoning is more pleasing to the Blessed Trinity and more honorable for man's salvation, without comparison, than ever Adam's sin was harmful."

In that truth we find the strength to believe that "just as by God's courtesy he forgets our sin from the time that we repent, just so does he wish us to forget our sins and all our depression and all our doubtful fears." That Gospel confidence anchors us in the Providence of God who promises: "I will make all things well, I shall make all things well, I may make all things well and I can make all things well; and you will see that yourself, that all things will be well" (confer *Catechism* 312). Even our sins and sufferings.

One idiosyncratic aspect of Julian's treatment is her reference to God as Mother. She writes: "As truly as God is our Father, so truly is God our Mother.... The high might of the Trinity is our Father, and the deep wisdom of the Trinity is our Mother." The *Catechism* verifies such insight where it teaches: "God's parental tenderness can also be expressed by the image of motherhood, which emphasizes God's immanence, the intimacy between Creator and creature." (239)

In another place Julian identifies this dimension with Jesus: "The second Person of the Trinity is our Mother.... All the lovely works and all the sweet, loving offices of beloved motherhood are appropriated to the second Person.... He is our Mother of mercy.... In our Mother Christ we profit and increase, and in mercy he reforms and restores us.... Our Mother works in mercy on all his beloved children who are docile and obedient to him, and grace works with mercy."

Jesus manifests maternal traits in his saving actions. As a mother carries her expectant child, so does the Lord carry his cross and us with him to his Passion and the New Life of Resurrection: "Our true Mother Jesus alone bears us for joy and for endless life.... So he carries us within him in love and travail, until the full time when he wanted to suffer the sharpest thorns and cruel pains." As a mother suckles her child, so does "our precious Mother Jesus feed us with himself with the Blessed Sacrament." As a mother holds her child tenderly to her breast, so does "our tender Mother Jesus lead us easily into his blessed breast through his sweet open side."

However, it is as an antidote to the power of sin that we best understand the maternal efficacy of Christ: "Often when our falling and our wretchedness are shown to us, we are so much afraid and so greatly ashamed of ourselves that we scarcely know where we can put ourselves. But then our courteous Mother does not wish us to flee away, for nothing would be less pleasing to him; but he then wants us to behave like a child. For when it is distressed and frightened, it runs quickly to its mother; and if it can do no more, it calls to the mother for help with all its might, saying: 'My beloved Mother, have mercy on me. I have made myself filthy and unlike you, and I cannot make it right except with your help and grace.'"

This understanding does not displace the Blessed Mother's own primacy in the Christian's sanctification. "Our Lady is our Mother in whom we are all enclosed and born of her in Christ, for she who is Mother of our Savior is Mother of all who are saved in our Savior." God makes Mary great, not for herself alone, but for us. "Jesus says: 'Do you wish to see in Mary how you are loved? It is for love of you that I have made her so exalted, so noble, so honorable; and this delights me. And I wish it to delight you.'" In the Blessed Mother, not only do we come to full awareness of how much God loves us, but also we find the perfect way for us to love and delight God in return. "God wishes it to be known that all who take delight in him should take delight in Mary, and in the delight that he has in her and she in him."

The Blessed Mother — like all the saints — does not impede but rather augments our intimacy with God. "It pleases God that we seek him and honor him through intermediaries, understanding and knowing that he is the goodness of everything…. The chief and principal intermediary is the blessed nature which Jesus took of the Virgin."

The Blessed Mother remains in the hearts of all fervent believers, for "every contemplative soul to whom it is given to look and to seek will see

Mary and pass on to God through contemplation."
Heartfelt meditation on "the virtues of her blessed
soul, her truth, her wisdom, her love" teaches us
to know ourselves and reverently to fear God.
Because of our union with Mary, we at last can
believe in the intensity of divine love for us which
proclaims: "It is a joy and a bliss and an endless
delight to me that ever I suffered my Passion for
you, for if I could suffer more, I would."

5

The Dialogue

The Vatican II *Pastoral Constitution on the Church in the Modern World* (*Gaudium et Spes*) reminds us that God reveals himself by revealing man to himself (41). But six centuries earlier another powerful Catholic voice was already asserting this same important truth. Her name is St. Catherine of Siena, a Dominican tertiary and Doctor of the Church. In the years 1377-78, two years before her death at age thirty-three, St. Catherine composed *The Dialogue*, a theological treatise meant to instruct, nurture, and inspire the faith-life of her various spiritual followers.

The Dialogue is so-named because of the conversational exchange between God and St. Catherine that forms the work. At the heart of this masterpiece is St. Catherine's teaching on self-knowledge. She refers to herself as a soul who "has become accustomed to dwelling in the cell of self-knowledge so as to know better the goodness of God toward her."

St. Catherine systematically explains the program of self-revelation by which the believer comes to recognize and grasp God who wishes to be known by his people. The process begins and ends in a disposition of humility that enables us to know God in ourselves. From that knowledge, St. Catherine reassures us, we will draw all that we need.

Humility, however, does not mean self-deprecation or condemnation. Rather, St. Catherine insists that before considering any personal limitation or shortcoming, we must first be mindful of the mercy of Jesus. In mystical dialogue, God says to her and to us: "I do not want the soul to think about her sins either in general or specifically without calling to mind the blood and the greatness of my mercy." Rather, all self-knowledge must be tempered by and with the knowledge of God alive within us. As the Lord relates in *The Dialogue*: "The soul should season her self-knowledge with knowledge of my goodness, and her knowledge of me with self-knowledge."

Neglect of that principle plunges us into both confusion and an unhealthy sorrow for our sins that leads to despair. The *Catechism of the Catholic Church* teaches that "without the knowledge Revelation gives of God we cannot recognize sin clearly." (387) Therefore, the Church adjures us to fasten onto God's love as both the motive for and means of undoing our sin. St. Catherine prays: "Who

am I, wretched as I am, that you, eternal Father
have revealed to me your truth and the delusion
of selfishness I can be subject to in this pilgrim
life?... Who moved you to this? Love! For you
loved me without being loved by me." As a result,
any attempt to assess our imperfection apart from
this priority fails because it violates God's plan.

Unfortunately, the devil relentlessly endeavors to make us think our sins are too great
for God. However, the Lord through his saint prescribes the necessary antidote for such pernicious
deception: "You must keep expanding your heart
and your affection in the immeasurable greatness
of my mercy, with true humility." That devotion
brings about in us the right kind of self-contempt
from which we draw knowledge of God's goodness as we begin to conform our will to God's
in a spirit of joy and compassion. Therefore, it is
incumbent upon the soul to safeguard simultane-
ously three truths: knowledge of self, knowledge of
God's goodness, and knowledge "that the medicine
by which God willed to heal the whole world is
humble, constant, holy prayer."

But why would God implement such a dynamic in the first place? The answer lies in God's
compassionate understanding of human nature. As
St. Catherine reminds us, those who do not know
themselves disable themselves from ever knowing
God or his justice in truth. Consequently, God sets
forth a sanctified strategy that leads all to perfect

self-knowledge as well as to a hope-filled shame over transgression by which they "may atone for their sins and placate God's wrath by humbly asking for mercy." St. Catherine's doctrine makes it clear that it is not severe penance that delights God but rather unflagging reliance on his mercy. That is how we best grow to understand God and ourselves in God's sight.

This holy dependency binds each believer as a participation in the central force that forms the very essence of the Church. God says to Catherine: "I have distributed my spiritual gifts in such a way that no one has all of them. I gave something to one person, something else to another, so that each one's need would be a reason to have recourse to the other. I wanted to make you dependent on one another so that each of you would be my minister dispensing the graces and gifts you have received from me." This truth impresses upon us that our every action affects the greater community with its repercussions. *The Dialogue* warns: "You cannot do good or evil for yourself without doing the same for your neighbors."

Such an atmosphere should curb the instance of selfishness, which St. Catherine calls the "breeding ground of all evil." But when it grows unweeded in people, it causes them to fail in constancy. Lack of perseverance in turn leads to presumption, as the Lord warns: "They accept my mercy and hope with great presumption. And presumptuous as they are, they put their trust in my mercy even while they are continually abusing it. They use my mercy as a weapon against me." Presumption darkens the mind's eye depriving us of the light of faith and of the ability to discern God's Providence.

The Dialogue refers to those who are so afflicted that they are as good as dead to grace: "Being dead they remember nothing of my mercy. They love nothing but what is dead." The counsel of a good spiritual director provides a way out of this hell by placing the fallen-away onto the Bridge who is Jesus. In this regard, St. Catherine prefers "a humble and unschooled person with a holy and up-right conscience" to a "well-read but proud scholar with great knowledge." For good spiritual directors are those who "share the light within them in hunger and longing for others' salvation."

That light helps the misguided to understand that "God is like one drunk with love for our good." God promises Catherine that his "goodness is never hidden from anyone who wants to receive it." What the Lord requires of us then is our ardent desire. For as the Lord relates: "I who am infinite God want you to serve me with what is infinite, and you have nothing infinite except your soul's love and desire." In turn, we receive God's light in proportion to the love and burning desire we bring to him.

God's request reveals his own utter lack of selfishness, for he instructs us: "I ask you to love me with the same love with which I love you."

God holds nothing back from us and expects nothing from us that we have not first received from him. This constitutes the special privilege of the redeemed, for it is a prerogative we in no way deserve: "These people do not trust me, though I want nothing other than their sanctification. They are always scandalized in me, and I support and bear with them in great patience because I loved them without their ever loving me."

Our reciprocation of divine love serves as the singular standard by which God blesses us with his favor: "Each of you will be rewarded according to the measure of your love, not according to your work or the time spent." Mysteriously though, God deepens his love by sharing with us the cross of his Son: "Suffering and sorrow increase in proportion to love." At the same time, weighty consequences attend those who allow their faith to weaken: "Because the redeemed owe me so much love, if they refuse it their sin is all the greater. Sin is punished far more severely after people have been redeemed by the blood than before."

In summary then, authentic holiness unceasingly recalls us to the Truth. The Father tells St. Catherine: "This is one reason why the wicked of the world do not change their ways: they do not believe in truth, by the light of living faith, that I see them. For if they believed they would not commit such evil but would turn away from what they have done and humbly ask for my mercy.

And I, through my Son's blood, would be merciful to them." These words reveal the most profound meaning of divine "providence": God constantly, actively, compassionately watches over us.

We are called to change precisely by placing our confidence in God's foresight and forgiveness. God wants us to know that he knows all about us. And when we accept that truth in the humility of right self-knowledge, God, who knows our ways, reveals his own ways to us: "My ways are known only to those who have the light. This light is won in the soul's knowledge of herself, which makes her rise above the darkness."

All of this helps us to understand why St. Catherine of Siena identifies both disobedience and thanklessness as the source of all evil. In the end, perhaps the best advice for us is to fulfill the simple command God gives to his saint: "Fall in love with my Providence!"

6

The Imitation of Christ

"Egotism, Materialism, Hedonism." This seems to be the slogan that typifies the temperament of the modern world. What can a fifteenth-century spiritual treatise possibly have to say to such a mindset? The answer: Everything.

The three central themes of *The Imitation of Christ* stand as the antithesis to the fixations of the contemporary psyche, and provide an antidote for them. Although the work attributed to Thomas à Kempis was originally written for a community of religious priests, its message reaches beyond that audience right into our present day malaise. It does so by teaching us authoritatively about true self-love, detachment, and suffering.

A prevalent trendy truism contends that, to insure psychological well-being, we must "love ourselves." Unfortunately, the popular bent interprets this claim as an excuse for indulgence, irresponsibility, and moral license. However, as à Kempis rightly points out: "From this vice of too much self-love comes almost every other vice that must be uprooted.... By loving myself badly I lost myself, by seeking only You and by truly loving You I have found both myself and You."

Self-love is crucial to personal wholeness and holiness. But true self-love finds its referent and its source outside of the self and in Jesus Christ. Rectified self-regard requires that we love ourselves the way God loves us. As such, we are not responsible for originating or inaugurating that love. Rather, self-love means allowing Jesus to love us first with his love, as à Kempis testifies: "Left to myself, I am nothing but total weakness. But if You look upon me for an instant, I am at once made strong and filled with new joy."

The key is giving ourselves to God right now just the way we are. Self-love quickens in us through the conviction that we are lovable solely because of the goodness of God. The only gift that God desires of us in this moment is our actual being with all its imperfection. God wants us to realize that he desires nothing from us that he has not first given us. "You are what you are, and you cannot be said to be better than you are in God's sight."

This obliges us to cease trying to convince ourselves of our own goodness. For everything that God wants to give us flows from his abundance and our nothingness. God demands nothing of us but to be permitted to make us perfect by his love.

He loves us by overcoming in us what we cannot overcome in ourselves.

Therefore, *The Imitation* stresses that we must love ourselves in the hatred of everything in us that is not of God. "You can never be perfectly free unless you completely renounce self, for all who seek their own interest and who love themselves are bound in fetters. They are unsettled by covetousness and curiosity, always searching for ease and not for the things of Christ, often devising and framing that which will not last, for anything that is not of God will fail completely."

The Imitation, then, teaches us that we truly please God by what we let him give us. The reward of that disposition is personal sanctification that remains out of the question by worldly standards: "Then all vain imaginations, all wicked disturbances and superfluous cares will vanish. Then also immoderate fear will leave you and inordinate love will die."

This path to holiness involves a daily dying to self. "The more you depart from yourself, the more you will be able to enter into me. As the giving up of exterior things brings interior peace, so the forsaking of self unites you to God." Which leads us to *The Imitation*'s second theme: detachment.

In the judgment of à Kempis, materialism is one of the chief impediments to the spiritual life. "The reason why so few contemplative persons are found is that so few know how to separate themselves entirely from what is transitory and created." Indeed, an undue preoccupation with possessions does violence to a person spiritually. "Nothing so mars and defiles the heart of man as impure attachment to created things."

Accordingly, *The Imitation* counsels: "Do not possess anything that can hinder you or rob you of freedom." For, despite the deceit of the world, the truth remains that "you cannot be satisfied with any temporal goods because you were not created to enjoy them." Ironically, legitimate delight in created things is itself the fruit of detachment: "Unless a person be elevated in spirit, free from all creatures, and completely united to God, all his knowledge and possessions are of little moment."

True happiness, however, consists in delighting in God, and "when a person reaches a point where he seeks no solace from any creature, then he begins to relish God perfectly."

That ongoing dedication to detachment constitutes a kind of suffering... the third theme. In the thinking of à Kempis, the purpose of suffering is to save us from presumption by showing us again and again how we have nothing of our own apart from God by which we can please God. He therefore consoles us in the voice of Christ: "Do not consider yourself forsaken if I send some temporary hardship, or withdraw the consolation you desire. For this is the way to the kingdom of heaven, and without doubt it is better for you and the rest of my servants to be tried in adversities than to have all things as you wish."

In fact, we can expect our sufferings to intensify as our intimacy with God deepens. For "the more spiritual progress a person makes, so much heavier will he frequently find the cross, because as his love increases, the pain of his exile also increases." But God honors even minute sufferings: "With God, nothing that is suffered for his sake, no matter how small, can pass without reward."

In the end, the spiritual program outlined in *The Imitation* remains ordered to one, exclusive goal: to lead the believer to a deeper love of Jesus for his own sake. It is an essential book for cutting through worldly subterfuge, and directing the Christian onto the certain path of peace. "A person who is a lover of Jesus and of truth, a truly interior person who is free from uncontrolled affections, can turn to God at will and rise above himself to enjoy spiritual peace."

7

The Spiritual Exercises

Ignatius of Loyola composed *The Spiritual Exercises* as a kind of manual to guide retreatants through the thirty day spiritual exercises under the counsel of a director. Completed in 1541, *The Spiritual Exercises* aim to help the retreatant "to overcome oneself, and to order one's life." In the process, they assist the director whose task is to "unmask the deceptive tactics of the enemy of our human nature."

By the term "spiritual exercises" St. Ignatius includes "every method of examination of conscience, meditation, contemplation, vocal or mental prayer, and other spiritual activities, i.e., any means of preparing and disposing our soul to rid itself of all its disordered affections and of seeking and finding God's will in the ordering of our life for the salvation of our soul." Ignatius' working principle for the *Exercises* is that "human beings are created to praise, reverence, and serve God our Lord, and by doing this to save their souls."

To this end, the saint urges all potential

retreatants to enter the *Exercises* "by offering all their desires and freedom to God so that his divine majesty can make use of their persons and of all they possess in whatsoever way is in accord with his most holy will." Each exercise begins with a "preparatory prayer" by which the retreatant asks God "for the grace that all my intentions, actions, and operations may be ordered purely to the service and praise of the Divine Majesty." In the fourth week of the *Exercises*, St. Ignatius offers his now-famous dedicatory prayer which reflects his foundational theme: "Take, Lord, and receive all my liberty, my memory, my understanding, and all my will — all that I have and possess. You, Lord, have given all that to me. I now give it back to you, O Lord. All of it is yours. Dispose of it according to your will. Give me love of yourself along with your grace, for that is enough for me."

By such self-donation, the retreatant allows the Creator to "communicate himself to the devout soul, embracing it in love and praise, and disposing it for the way which will enable the soul to serve him better in the future." This is the reason for undertaking the *Exercises*: "to desire and choose only that which is more conducive to the end for which we are created." In the process, St. Ignatius wants us to grasp that "what fills and satisfies the soul consists, not in knowing much, but in our understanding the realities profoundly and in savoring them interiorly."

Ignatius focuses our attention on four crucial realities during the four weeks of retreat. The first week is devoted to a reflective consideration of sinfulness; the second, to the life of Jesus up to Palm Sunday; the third, to the Passion; and the fourth to the Resurrection and Ascension. So as to benefit fully from these meditations, Ignatius instructs the retreatant to "remain for a full hour in each of the five exercises or contemplations which will be made each day." Such intense devotion helps counteract the common experience of being "tempted grossly and openly." The saint also counsels seclusion in order "to enjoy a freer use of our natural faculties for seeking diligently what we so ardently desire." He recognizes a valuable practical advantage in solitude: "The more we keep ourselves alone and secluded, the more fit do we make ourselves to approach and attain to our Creator and Lord; and the more we unite ourselves to him in this way the more do we dispose ourselves to receive graces and gifts from his divine and supreme goodness."

The Spiritual Exercises direct the retreatant to make an examination of conscience three times a day. There are five points to the Ignatian method: thank God for benefits received; ask for the grace to know our sins and to rid ourselves of them; ask an account of our souls; ask pardon of God for our faults; and finally, resolve to amend our failings with God's grace. Ignatius realizes that "during these spiritual exercises one reaches a deeper interior understanding of the reality and malice of one's sins than when one is not so concentrated on interior concerns." Therefore, Ignatius makes it a priority "to know and grieve for our sins more deeply" during the time of retreat so as to receive greater profit and merit. At the same time, the retreatant performs exterior penances to satisfy for past sins, to overcome self, and "to seek and obtain some grace or gift or to obtain a solution to some doubt in which one finds oneself."

Certain important themes punctuate the *Exercises*. Humility logically occupies a central place in Ignatian spirituality. The saint notes three ways of being humble. The first way involves lowering ourselves so as to become obedient to the law of God in all things. The second and better way of humility calls for a conversion of our desires so that we do not feel "strongly attached to having wealth rather than poverty, or honor rather than dishonor, or a long life rather than a short one. Furthermore, neither for all creation nor to save my life would I ever reach a decision to commit a venial sin." The most perfect way of humility impels us to "choose poverty with Christ poor rather than wealth; contempt with Christ laden with it rather than honors. Even further, I desire to be regarded as a useless fool for Christ, who before me was regarded as such, rather than as a wise or prudent person in this world."

As a natural consequence to such humility,

retreatants may experience a profound vulnerability in which the "evil spirit" works "to cause gnawing anxiety, to sadden, and to set up obstacles. In this way he unsettles these persons by false reasons aimed at preventing their progress." Of course, we can bring on such desolation ourselves by being "tepid, lazy, or negligent in our spiritual exercises." Yet, we should not disregard how God uses these struggles for our good. He may allow spiritual desolation "to test how much we are worth and how far we will extend ourselves in the service and praise of God." Desolation strips us of "pride and vainglory," bestowing upon us a graced recognition that "we cannot by ourselves bring on or retain great devotion, intense love, tears, or any other spiritual consolation, but that all these are a gift and grace from God."

Ignatius counsels the one in desolation "to preserve himself or herself in patience. After awhile the consolation will return again." Spiritual trials can be countered "by insisting more on prayer, meditation, earnest self-examination, and some suitable way of doing penance." However, once consolation returns, St. Ignatius the realist warns that one "should consider how he or she will act in future desolation, and store up new strength for that time."

Ignatius of Loyola is not vague about the impact of the devil in the life of the believer: "There is no beast on the face of the earth as fierce as the enemy of human nature when he is pursuing his damnable intention with his surging malice." He exposes the devil's seductive and duplicitous ways: "The enemy acts like a false lover, insofar as he tries to remain secret and undetected." The enemy preys on our human tendency to hide in our sins: "When the enemy of human nature turns his wiles and persuasions upon an upright person, it intends and desires them to be received and kept in secrecy." In all this, the devil wants to fight against any happiness and spiritual joy that God deems to give us. Therefore, Ignatius counsels the retreatant to stand "bold and unyielding against the enemy's temptations" so as to weaken and discourage the devil in a way that puts him to flight.

The Blessed Mother plays an essential role in our effort to grow in graced perfection. St. Ignatius directs the individual retreatant to ask Mary for three things: "First, that I may feel an interior knowledge of my sins and also an abhorrence of them; Second, that I may perceive the disorder in my actions, in order to detest them, amend myself, and put myself in order; Third, that I may have a knowledge of the world, in order to detest it and rid myself of all that is worldly and vain."

In a critical way, the Church supports us in this endeavor. By relying on certain teachers of the faith like St. Thomas Aquinas, we benefit from their wisdom. For "they, being enlightened and clarified by divine influence, make profitable use of the councils, canons, and decrees of our Holy Mother Church." By our faithfulness to the Church we grow in intimacy with the Holy Spirit, for by "the same Spirit and Lord of ours who gave the ten commandments our Holy Mother Church is guided and governed."

In short, the spiritual exercises enable the retreatants to know how much the Lord desires to give us "even his very self." They dispose us to value "above everything else the great service which is given to God because of pure love." In the fourth week, the retreatants ask for interior knowledge of all the great good they have received so that, moved to profound thankfulness, they may "become able to love and serve the Divine Majesty in all things." Therefore, we wholeheartedly give ourselves to this service, confident that "the more one divests oneself of self-love, self-will, and self-interests, the more progress one will make."

8

The Ascent of Mount Carmel

Of the many teachers of ascetical theology who have appeared on the scene since the sixteenth century, one master whose voice continues to resound is St. John of the Cross. Here was a holy man who truly lived what he taught. In 1577, after refusing to renounce his support of a reform of the Carmelite Order, John of the Cross was imprisoned in a closet-like room by other Carmelite friars. In this windowless, six by ten foot dungeon, John of the Cross subsisted on bread, water, and sardines. Three times a week he endured a communally administered flagellation in the refectory geared to make him recant.

It did not work. Instead, after eight months of cruel incarceration, John of the Cross managed to escape to safety. The next year he began work on his masterpiece of mystical theology, *The Ascent of Mount Carmel*, which he completed in 1585. This combination of lived experience and mystical insight makes for a compelling spiritual doctrine that cannot be ignored.

John of the Cross intended his book principally for certain friars and nuns of the Order of the Primitive Observance of Mount Carmel who were especially interested in spiritual perfection. However, he broadened the scope of the work to accommodate the spiritual advancement of anyone who might read it.

The purpose of the book, in St. John's words, is to explain "how to reach divine union quickly." This high state of perfection is symbolized by the summit of Mount Carmel, which the author presents in an annotated diagram at the start of his treatise.

The text of *The Ascent* stands as a commentary on John of the Cross's classic poem about spiritual perfection which opens the book. The soul in the poem who departs from his stilled house represents everyone seeking ultimate union with God. That stillness symbolizes the renunciation and mortification of the appetites required of one on the road ascending to God. The author insists that every soul must be purified in order to undertake this journey, for only such a purgation puts to flight the devil who wields power over a person attached to temporal and bodily things.

Earthly attachments afflict the soul in multiple ways: they stir the passions to combat and control the soul; they "fasten the spirit to earth and do not allow it freedom of heart"; they empty the soul of the spirit and joy of God; they cripple the soul's ability to possess God; they deprive the soul of "the enlightenment and dominating fullness of God's pure and simple light." Attachments manage to deceive and manipulate the soul. The unsurrendered will "easily finds joy in what deserves no rejoicing, hope in what brings it no profit, sorrow over what should cause rejoicing, and fear where there is no reason for fear."

St. John emphasizes the mollycoddle character of the appetites: "The appetites are wearisome and tiring. They resemble little children, restless and hard to please, always whining to their mother for this thing or that, and never satisfied." Therefore, he instructs us to strive for purity in the measure of our natural capacity, for such purgation enables the kind of personal nakedness and emptiness required to bring about true peace, satisfaction, and union with God.

Inattention to attachments — even slight ones — can cause us to forfeit all. The saint implores us, then, to prepare for our union with God, not through understanding, feeling, or imagining, but through purifying love "which is the stripping off and perfect renunciation of all experiences for God." Gospel love means "to labor to divest and deprive oneself for God of all that is not God."

This process of "disencumbering, emptying, and depriving the faculties of their natural rights and operations" makes room for "the inflow and illumination of the supernatural." Such a level of divine communication becomes possible only once one "turns his eyes from his natural capacity." God longs for us to possess him in a way that exceeds our limitations, as the *Catechism* teaches: "God wishes to make men capable of responding to him, and of knowing him, and of loving him far beyond their own natural capacity." (52)

However, once the appetites become mortified and attachments extinguished, transformation occurs. At this point, St. John alerts us, "the soul appears to be God more than a soul." This soul "will possess all that God himself has." One's vigilant avoidance of small attachments prevents him from falling into greater ones. The faithful's non-possessive spirit liberates him for authentic rejoicing in God's creatures. Constant detachment provides an infallible standard for monitoring one's relationship with God: "The illumination of the soul and its union with God corresponds to the measure of its purity." It enables the soul to "walk out to genuine freedom to the enjoyment of union with its Beloved." It is for this that God creates us, as the *Catechism* makes clear: "Man lives a fully human life only if he freely lives by his bond with God." (44)

At the same time, once the soul no longer feeds on the pleasure of the appetites, he begins to live "in a void and in darkness" leaning on pure faith alone. St. John identifies faith, not as knowledge derived from the senses, but as "an assent of the soul to what enters through hearing." It is a "dark night" that paradoxically gives light.

The Ascent observes that "all that can be grasped by the intellect would serve as an obstacle rather than a means if a person were to become attached to it." We are warned that "any person desiring some vision or revelation would be guilty of offending God by not fixing his eyes entirely upon Christ and by living with the desire for some other novelty." This is why St. John instructs that a soul "must advance to union with God's wisdom by unknowing rather than by knowing... by blinding itself and remaining in darkness."

Such an approach secures several advantages for the soul. The darkness of faith cloaks and protects the soul: "The person who walks in faith is concealed and hidden from the devil.... Because of this disguise, neither temporal nor rational things recognize or detain it.... Faith is comparable to midnight." Blind faith invests us with a spirit of confident patience, for God "promises many things, not so that there be an immediate understanding of them, but that afterwards at the proper time one may receive light about them." This way of knowing endows us with the most sublime knowledge which, John of the Cross tells us, "consists in a certain touch of divinity."

Hope, too, undergoes transformation via detachment. In St. John's thought, hope is ordered to begetting "an emptiness of possessions in the memory" which converts us from a fixation on the past to true confidence in the future. Too often our own condemning memories keep us from believing in the promise of God's mercy and grace for us. Therefore, "in the beginning, when union with God is in the process of being perfected, a person cannot but experience great forgetfulness of all things, since forms and knowledge are gradually being erased from the memory." The divine union effectively sweeps away every harmful recollection, thereby elevating the memory to the supernatural. "In the measure that the memory becomes dispossessed of things it will have hope."

Each believer plays a part in the process of purging the memory so as to live in pure hope: "As often as distinct ideas, forms, and images occur to him, he should immediately, without resting in them, turn to God with loving affection, in emptiness of everything rememberable." This detachment from the allure of memory increases our ability to hope in God alone, and "the more a soul hopes the more it attains." Then God's spirit makes us "know what must be known and ignore what must be ignored, remember what ought to be remembered and forget what ought to be forgotten."

Divine love, too, comes from such self-purging: "A man must strip himself of all creatures and of his actions and abilities so that when everything unlike and unconformed to God is cast out, his soul may receive the likeness of God, and thus be transformed in God." Divine intimacy, then, involves three key aspects: conformity, equality, and likeness. It requires relinquishing our hold on our will so as to insure authentic conformity to the will of God. This conformity obliges us "to choose for love of Christ all that is most distasteful whether in God or in the world — and such is the love of God."

At the same time, love effects equality, for in loving another we make ourselves as low as the other, "and in some way even lower." Love equates by subjecting the lover to the loved one. God himself is the first one to accede to this dynamic: "In order that God lift the soul from the extreme of its low state to the other extreme of the high state of divine union, he must do so with order, gently, and according to the mode of the soul. He begins by communicating spirituality in accord with the person's littleness and small capacity." In such compassion and condescension the profound depth of God's love becomes clear.

The effect of this charity is a similarity between lover and the one loved that John of the Cross calls the "union of likeness." He defines it as a transformation of the soul in God where there is likeness of love. In turn, this union remains singularly efficacious in all the believer's actions. St. John reminds us that "the value of the Christian's good works is not based upon their quantity and quality so much as upon the love of God practiced in them. They are deeper in quality the purer and more entire the love of God is by which they are performed." The likeness of love that we share with God, then, endows us with the privilege of revealing the very essence of divine love to the world. In turn, the Lord protects and sustains the faithful in that relationship: "God's Spirit makes them love what they ought to love, and keeps them from loving what is not in God."

Ironically, this vigilant attention to self-renunciation in no way leaves us isolated. "God will not bring clarification and confirmation of the truth to the heart of one who is alone. Such a person would remain weak and cold in regard to truth." On the contrary, the ascent to divine union draws us into the very heart and life of the Church.

Our humble approach to faith, hope, and love purifies us of every prideful or pretentious inclination in dealing with God. Instead, the believer delights to rely on the counsel and direction of other believers. St. John emphasizes: "God is desirous of this, for to declare and strengthen truth on the basis of natural reason, he draws near those who come together in an endeavor to know it."

Prayer stands as the chief means of advancing the union between the faithful and God. "The soul should learn to remain in God's presence with a loving attention and tranquil intellect, even though he seems to himself to be idle." In other words, the soul departs from his stilled house in order to enter into the mystical stillness of God. *The Ascent* assures that "at that moment it recollects itself in the presence of God, it enters upon an act of general, loving, peaceful, and tranquil knowledge, drinking wisdom and love and delight."

Part of that knowledge includes insight about other people's needs. "God sometimes shows holy souls the necessities of their neighbors so that through their prayer he may provide a remedy." Such solicitude can extend even to strangers: "At times God will give the soul a desire to pray for others whom it has never known nor heard." And this is just as it should be. For in that anonymous albeit actual union with others in prayer, we receive a living sign of our ultimate union with God.

9

Interior Castle

The great Doctor of the Church St. Teresa of Avila did not want to write her masterpiece *Interior Castle*. She undertook the project in a spirit of obedience that entailed great difficulty for her: "I do not feel that the Lord has given me either the spiritual power or the desire for it." But write she does for the nuns of the Carmelite Order who in 1577 needed "someone to solve their difficulties about prayer. It is to them that I am writing." Ironically, St. Teresa did not foresee the major contribution her treatise would make to all the Church, for she considered ridiculous and absurd "the idea that anyone else could benefit by what I say."

The fruit of her modesty is a classic work that describes the degrees of spiritual life and growth according to the image of a castle: "Think of the soul as resembling a castle... containing many mansions. You must not imagine these mansions as rooms placed in succession, but fix your eyes on the center, the court inhabited by the King.... This principal room is surrounded by many others."

The first mansion is a place of darkness since "the light that comes from the King's palace hardly reaches it at all." When the soul enters this mansion, many bad things accompany it — "snakes, vipers and venomous reptiles." These evil creatures prevent the soul from seeing and enjoying whatever light is in the room. The "wild beasts" blind the soul to everything but themselves.

The darkness and the dangers of the first mansion symbolize "the condition of a soul that is so worldly and preoccupied with earthly riches, honors, and affairs that, even if it sincerely wishes to enjoy the beauties of the castle, it is prevented by these distractions."

Such souls cannot free themselves from plaguing impediments. Therefore, they must "as often as possible have recourse to God's majesty, taking the Blessed Mother and the saints for their advocates to do battle for them." By such prayer and meditation we eventually gain access to the inner mansion. For that devotion produces in us the prerequisite self-knowledge otherwise impossible to attain "unless we seek to know God."

Once we realize the importance of getting out of the first mansion and we demonstrate that conviction in a habit of regular prayer, we make our way to the second mansion. However, the dwellers here lack firm resolution as they still subject themselves to the occasions of sin.

These souls possess definite advantages. They are in less peril than those in the first mansion. They better comprehend their position which impels them in hope to progress to the castle. They understand the Lord when he calls them, and they revere him as a "good neighbor."

But here souls suffer more than in the preceding mansion. For with "the understanding being more vigilant and the powers more on the alert" now the devil can cunningly persuade them "that the world and its joys are almost eternal." Even if a soul manifests a readiness to make further spiritual progress, "all hell will league together to force it to turn back."

How then does one triumph in this mansion? First of all, we must not harbor expectations of spiritual favors: "Souls who act thus will continually suffer from discouragement and temptations." Secondly, we must welcome our struggles: "Bad thoughts and aridities are often permitted by God to assail and torment us so that we cannot repel them; and sometimes he even allows these reptiles to bite us to teach us to be more on our guard in the future and to see whether we grieve much at offending him." Thirdly, we must seek out holy companions in the faith since "it is of the utmost importance for a person to associate with those who lead a spiritual life." Fourthly, we must never abandon our striving to grow in knowledge of ourselves, for "it would be madness to think that we could get to heaven without sometimes retiring into our souls so as to know ourselves, or thinking of our failings and of what we owe to God, or frequently imploring his mercy."

For the process of sanctification is a slow and lengthy one, which is not a problem for God who "is willing to wait for us many a day and even many a year, especially when he sees perseverance and good desires in our hearts." Therefore, neither should we make it a problem for ourselves, but rather give ourselves patiently to prayer: "The habit of recollection is not to be gained by force of arms, but with calmness."

Those who through fortitude and perseverance enter the third mansion receive a very great favor from the Lord. However, we must not spoil this good beginning by believing that we deserve something from God. Humility and resoluteness of will are required here where our awareness of personal progress threatens to lead us to presumption. For often God withdraws his help from souls in order to make them conscious of the misery of their shortcomings. This shows us something of our perduring pettiness, our attachment, and our self-sufficiency. "I consider that God thus shows them great mercy, for though their behavior may be faulty, yet they gain greatly in humility." It spurs us on to a more ardent love: "How I wish love were strong enough to overcome reasons so that we might not be content to creep on our way to God." But this is not a place where God gives many consolations beyond a preparatory glimpse at what is happening in the remaining mansions.

In the fourth mansion we "begin to encounter the supernatural.... I believe this mansion to be the one most souls enter. As the natural is combined with the supernatural, the devil can do more harm here than later on." For this reason, souls here must exert the greatest care to keep themselves from every occasion of sin. Rather, "the soul must continue receiving God's favors continually, for it is on their frequent reception that the whole welfare of the soul depends."

As the soul draws nearer to the dwelling of the King, she is so overwhelmed by the great beauty of the place that human understanding remains incapable of describing it. Consequently, as St. Teresa reminds us, "it is not so essential to think much as to love much." That love consists in "the fervent determination to strive to please God in all things" and to "love God without any motive of self-interest."

At this stage, God teaches souls "to recognize his voice and no longer wander, but return, like lost sheep." The divine consolation known as the Prayer of Quiet attunes our hearing to God's voice, for through it "the will must in some way be united with that of God." This prayer aids in the principal work of the will: "to realize its unworthiness to receive so great a good and to occupy itself in thanking God for it." For the first time the soul actually begins to desire trials so as to satisfy "a great desire to do something for God's sake."

"Riches, treasures and joys are contained in the fifth mansion," and "the majority manage to gain admittance." Here neither imagination nor memory nor understanding can impede. Here our close contact with God forbids even the devil to enter.

This place is characterized by an overwhelming certainty that God has implanted himself in the center of our soul. Here the soul "has so entirely yielded itself into God's hands that it knows or cares for nothing but that God should dispose of it according to his will."

Several fruits distinguish this mansion. The soul yearns to progress in faith: "Love is never idle, therefore it is a very bad sign when one comes to a stand-still in virtue." In addition, the soul manifests a mature detachment from every creature. It also possesses peace to such a high degree that even severe trials become a source of contentment. And God does send suffering so that the soul may be convinced that it belongs to him. Prayer keeps it constantly in our minds that without the presence of God "we would fall at once into the abyss."

In the sixth mansion the soul is completely determined to take no other spouse but God, and it seeks to be alone with him in renunciation of everything else. These souls enjoy a knowledge of

God's greatness, true self-knowledge and humility, and a supreme contempt for earthly things. The soul experiences a profound forgetfulness of self, and "death is ardently longed for."

All this is compounded by the great trials and severe distress souls in the mansion suffer. "Such spiritual dryness ensues that the mind feels as if it never had thought of God nor ever will be able to do so." As a remedy, St. Teresa prescribes occupying oneself with external affairs and works of charity. For "in such a tempest there is no other remedy except to wait for the mercy of God who, unexpectedly, by some casual word or unforeseen circumstance, suddenly dispels all these sorrows." In the process, holy souls recognize that "sorrow for sin increases in proportion to the divine grace received."

But there is profound consolation for the soul in this mansion: "Our Lord would have all people know that this soul is his own and that none may molest it, for it is all his. People are welcome to attack, if they will, the body, the honor, and the possessions of such a person, but the soul they must not assail; unless by a most culpable presumption it withdraws from the protection of its Spouse, he will defend it against the whole world and against all hell besides."

St. Teresa calls the seventh mansion a second heaven where God abides in the center of our souls. "This mansion differs from the rest in that the dryness and disturbance felt in all the rest at times hardly ever enter here where the soul is nearly always calm."

The soul is ushered into this mansion by means of an intellectual vision that enables the soul to see and understand something of the favor God grants it. In this state the soul carefully refrains from committing even the slightest sin. However, these souls recognize that "the Lord does not care so much for the importance of our works as for the love with which they are done." For God himself will unite our sacrifice with that which Jesus offered to the Father for us on the cross "so that they may be worth the value given them by our love."

We can summarize St. Teresa of Avila's doctrine from the point of view of the will in this program of spiritual maturity. The soul enters the first mansion with a will consumed by self-indulgence. It experiences some growth in the second mansion, yet the will continues to display a certain lack of steadfastness. Only in the third mansion does the soul begin to manifest the first signs of some resoluteness of will. In the fourth mansion for the first time does the soul experience her will being united with the divine will in prayer. There is a more perfect conformity of desires in the fifth mansion so that the soul wills what God wills to do with it. In the sixth mansion the soul offers the total renunciation of its entire will for God. And finally in the seventh mansion, the soul's will accrues to it new value as it is united in Christ's Passion.

Ironically, what the progression of *Interior Castle* points out is that the more we strive to arrive at God's abode, the more we discover that he truly dwells within us. Once the self-absorption of the first mansion gives way to grace, we become liberated truly to see and enjoy God in ourselves.

10

Introduction to the Devout Life

St. Francis de Sales once wrote: "There is no clock, no matter how good it may be, that doesn't need resetting and rewinding twice a day, once in the morning and once in the evening." Because that quaint custom today no longer applies, many might feel inclined to abandon the reality it signifies: pious devotion.

Yet, despite the outdatedness of the analogy and awesome advances in technology, the truthfulness of the insight continues to adhere: our relationship with God requires the constant attention of well-formed devotion that insures our growth in holiness. No kind of technology can supply that for us.

For this reason Francis de Sales, the bishop of Geneva and future Doctor of the Church, wrote his *Introduction to the Devout Life* in 1609. The saint defines his purpose: "to instruct those who live in town, within families, or at court, who, on the pretext of some supposed impossibility, will not even think of undertaking a devout life." Perhaps our reasons for neglecting devotion are different from the Christians of the seventeenth century. Nonetheless, de Sales endeavors "by this treatise to provide some assistance to those who with a generous heart" do undertake the project of a devout life.

The author anticipates the scorn brought on by a devotion to God: "As soon as worldly people see that you wish to follow a devout life they aim a thousand darts of mockery and even detraction at you." Yet, the saint adjures us to continue "to practice the ordinary, necessary actions that bring us to the love of God." In further instructing us, de Sales doesn't propose to present anything new, but rather "what has already been published by our predecessors on the same subject. It has been fashioned in a different order and way."

By devotion, St. Francis de Sales means "that spiritual ability and vivacity by which charity works in us or by aid of which we work quickly and lovingly. It is charity that makes us do good carefully, frequently, and promptly." Since it presupposes love of God, genuine devotion can be described simply as "true love of God." Such love naturally makes us devoted and devout for "we become like the things we love."

Perhaps Francis de Sales' chief insight is that authentic devotion is achieved by being acutely attuned both to nature and the supernatural. He writes: "To live a devout life you must not only cease to sin but you must also purify your heart of all affection for sin.... Base affections weaken your spirits so that it will be impossible to do good works promptly, diligently, and frequently."

The benefits of a devout life number many. Devotion first of all enables the Christian "to observe God's commandments more quickly and diligently." It also "perfects all things," adorning and beautifying every vocation. As a reward for devotion, "God will give you sufficient leisure and strength to perform all your other duties," for "we always do enough when God works with us." And it sees the good of God's providence at work in every moment, for "devotion makes honor and contempt alike useful to us."

In order to assist the reader's progress in the devout life, Francis de Sales provides a series of meditations that make up the bulk of the book. They aim to assist "in rooting out of your heart both sin and the chief affections for it." The first meditation provides the foundation and principle for all the rest: "God has drawn you out of nothingness to make you what you now are, and he has done so solely out of his own goodness. ... God has placed you in this world not because he needs you in any way — you are altogether useless to him — but only to exercise his own goodness in you by giving you his grace and glory." This same truth serves as the very cornerstone of the *Catechism of the Catholic Church*: "God, infinitely perfect and blessed in himself, in a plan of sheer goodness freely created man to make him share in his own blessed life." (1)

Francis de Sales is keenly aware of the way temptation can scourge the soul intent on devotion. Therefore, he wants us to be certain about how it fits into God's plan: "God permits violent assaults only in souls whom he desires to raise up to his own pure and surpassing love. By strong temptations God declares that he wants to make you great in his sight, but that you must always be humble and self-fearful."

Since God is not offended by temptations, neither should we be. The *Introduction* offers four constructive ways of responding to temptation. Following his penchant for animal imagery, de Sales instructs us not to engage temptation. Rather, "as soon as you are conscious of being tempted, follow the example of children when they see a wolf or bear out in the country. They immediately run to the arms of their father or mother for help and protection. Turn in the same way to God and implore his mercy and help."

We must unite ourselves to the cross in the midst of every temptation: "Observe the nature of the temptation and turn your heart gently toward Jesus Christ crucified and lovingly kiss his sacred feet.... If you find that the temptation still continues or even increases, run in spirit to embrace the Holy Cross as if you saw Christ Jesus crucified before you."

The third cure for temptation involves taking counsel: "The sovereign remedy against all temptation, whether great or small, is to open your heart and express its suggestions, feelings, and affections to your director." Secrecy spawned by guilt or shame is deadly: "The first condition the evil one makes with a soul he desires to seduce is for it to keep silence."

And the final technique for dealing with temptation takes us to the very heart of devotion: "Be content with quietly removing temptations. Do this by performing some actions of a contrary character, especially acts of love of God." For often, temptations — even little ones — may be blessings in disguise: "It may be that we will profit more by resisting small temptations. Wolves and bears are certainly more dangerous than flies but don't give us as much trouble or try our patience as much." And, as the saint assures us, "the more perfect our patience, the more completely do we possess our souls."

At the same time, we must not rush our developing relationship with God that Francis de Sales compares to "the dawning day which at its approach does not drive out the darkness instantaneously but only little by little." Not surprisingly, spiritual aridity may accompany us in our spiritual awakening… and sometimes it is of our own making. "It is ourselves who are often the cause of our own sterile, arid state." Self-indulgence leads directly to spiritual dryness: "You have glutted yourself with worldly pleasures and it is no wonder that spiritual delights disgust you." At times aridity is prompted by our presumption: "God holds back consolations from us when we have a foolish complacence in them." Our lack of heartfelt thankfulness also can cause aridity: "When we neglect to gather the dear delights of God's love at the proper season, he takes them from us." That is why the *Introduction* counsels us: "Marvel at your own ingratitude — a general sin that reaches out to all the rest and makes them infinitely more enormous."

The antidote for aridity is much like that for temptation: "Humble yourself greatly before God in recognition of your own nothingness and misery. Call on God and beg him for comfort. Go to your confessor, open your heart to him. There is nothing so profitable and fruitful in such states of aridity and sterility as not to have too much longing and desire for release from them. In this way we give ourselves up to God's pure mercy and special providence so that he may use us to serve him among such thorny and deserted places as long as he wishes to do so." On a practical note, de Sales suggests: "Perform fervent external actions even though it may be without relish, such as embracing the crucifix.... Sometimes you can arouse your heart by some act or movement of exterior devotion."

Such behavior saves us from anxiety, which Francis de Sales considers the second greatest evil that can happen to a soul. That anxiety — along with sloth, wrath, jealousy, envy, and impatience — occurs when sorrow for our spiritual state becomes disordered. We must not be deceived regarding our ability to do something about our aridity. "Among many persons, the great mistake is made of believing that the services we perform for God without relish are less agreeable to his divine Majesty. On the contrary, works performed in times of aridity are sweeter and become more precious in God's sight." In fact, devout acts performed despite an untender heart may be our only hope, even at critical moments, e.g.: "Once chastity is broken, nothing can preserve it except extraordinary devotion."

If genuine devotion is the same as true love of God, then the essence of the devout life is prayer. St. Francis de Sales' understanding of our urgent need for prayer is the fruit of his assessment of the condition of human nature: "Because of the frailty and evil inclinations of the flesh, our nature as men easily forgets its good dispositions. The flesh rests heavily on the soul and constantly drags it downward unless the soul frequently lifts itself up by fervent resolutions. You must often renew and repeat your good resolutions to serve God so that you don't neglect them and slip back into your former state or rather into one far worse." Prayer, then, "effectively purifies our intellect of ignorance and our will of depraved affections" by placing us in the brilliance of God's light and in the warmth of his heavenly love.

In addition to fervent prayer, healthy recreation contributes to the strength of the devout life. Foremost in this regard is the building up of spiritual friendship "by which two, three, or more souls establish a single spirit among themselves." Such friendship is central since "the delicious balm of devotion is distilled from one heart into another" and because "God is more glorified by the union and contribution of our good works with those of our brethren and neighbors." The ever-practical spiritual doctor prescribes "some kind of lawful relief and recreation" with others as a curative for aridity. He includes in his list of approved games tennis, charging the ring, chess, and backgammon. No matter what form it takes, it is important that we recreate: "It is a defect to be so strict, ill-bred, uncouth, and austere as neither to take any recreation ourselves nor to allow it to others."

Therefore, although technology advances by leaps and bounds, the human heart remains the same. That is why the Christian "must often reflect on his condition in order to reform and improve it. He must take it apart and examine every piece in detail: every affection and passion, in order to repair whatever defects there may be." For, as devout as we may desire to be, Jesus himself is first and foremost truly devoted to us: "On the tree of the Cross, the Heart of Jesus, our beloved, beheld your heart and loved it."

The Practice of the Presence of God

Not from the lofty stature of the pulpit or the lecture hall, but rather from his menial place in the monastery kitchen and shoe-repair shop does Brother Lawrence of the Resurrection expound his masterpiece of spirituality that has come to be called *The Practice of the Presence of God*. We owe its publication to Brother Lawrence's abbot who collected and edited the various writings of this French Carmelite after his death in 1691 for the monk's many friends, admirers, and inquirers.

Brother Lawrence's spiritual doctrine stems directly from his own lived faith. At age eighteen, Brother Lawrence was given a moving experience of God's love that, witnesses claim, sustained him for forty-odd years. The experience filled him with the resolve "to make the love of God the end of all his actions." Not that his life then became perfect. One acquaintance recalls that he was "a clumsy lummox who broke everything." For ten years he endured great suffering: "The apprehension of not being with God as I wished, my sins constantly on my mind and the great graces which God constantly showered on me, were the cause and source of all my difficulties."

However, despite the intensity of his trials, Brother Lawrence "knew by his faith that God was infinitely greater than whatever else he felt." He explains how it seemed that "man, reason and even God himself were against me and that only faith was for me." But at a critical moment, Brother Lawrence was blessed with a transforming grace: "Just as I thought I must live out my life beset by these difficulties and anxieties, I suddenly found myself changed and my soul experienced a profound interior peace as if it had found its center and a place of peace." Brother Lawrence had discovered the practice of the presence of God.

Brother Lawrence promotes the presence of God as "the holiest, most common, most necessary practice in the spiritual life." He defines it as a holy habit by which we "take delight in and become accustomed to God's divine company, speaking humbly and talking lovingly with him at all times, at every moment, without rule or system and especially in times of temptation, suffering, spiritual aridity, disgust and even of unfaithfulness and sin." In another place he describes it as a "simple attentiveness and a loving gaze upon God which I can call the actual presence of God, an habitual, silent and secret conversation of the soul with God."

This union through dialogue with God takes place "in the deepest recesses and the very center of the soul; it is here that the soul talks with God heart to heart, and always in a most sublime peace in which the soul rejoices in God." It comes about by applying our spirit to God "either by the imagination or by understanding." In this way, the practice of the presence of God "encompasses the whole spiritual life," and it assures that "whoever practices it correctly will soon attain the spiritual life." Brother Lawrence goes so far as to assert that this practice is the most pleasing "mode of life in the world" since it is "the life and nourishment of the soul."

Brother Lawrence provides a number of practical principles for this practice. He notes that "in the beginning, a persistent effort is needed to form the habit of continually talking to God." This initial difficulty comes from distracting thoughts that "spoil everything." Therefore, "we must be careful to reject them as soon as we perceive they are not necessary to our salvation, and resume again our conversation with God wherein we attain our greatest well being." This practice, then, requires as a prerequisite great purity of life. It demands great faithfulness to the "interior gaze on God" that is reinforced through the utterance of short ejaculations directed to God. And it relies on mortification whereby "the heart is emptied of all other things, for God wishes to possess it alone."

Yet, even if we stray a bit from the divine presence, "God makes himself felt" in our souls to recall us to him.

This practice produces several beneficial effects. It liberates us from what frightens us, for "while I am thus with God I fear nothing." It gives us authoritative power over the forces of evil: "By this continual mindfulness of God we shall crush the head of the devil and cause his weapons to fall from his hands." In turn, the practice greatly aids in the restoration of God's image within us: "These interior retreats to God gradually free us by destroying that self-love which can exist only among our fellow human beings." The practice elevates the believer's relationship with God: "The very heart of his soul, with no effort on his part, is raised up above all things and stays suspended and held there in God as in its center and its place of rest." It deepens our union with God, enlivening our faith, strengthening and increasing our hope, and inflaming our love by producing "in the heart a holy ardor, a sacred eagerness and a fervent desire to see this God." Because of our fervent practice of the presence of God, we "always see God and his glory in everything we do, say, and undertake."

Such devotion to God's presence directly affects the way we pray. It focuses our prayer life since the practice makes it "easy to keep your mind under control during your prayers or at least to keep it from wandering." It persuades us to "act

very simply with God and to speak with him
frankly." Therefore, we are not to underestimate
even "the least little remembrance" of God, for all
interior acts of adoration, "short though they may
be, are nevertheless very pleasing to God."

The facility of this form of prayer obliges
us to remain united with God at every moment,
whether we are at prayer itself or at work. Brother
Lawrence recommends this simple offering of the
heart over spiritual rules and particular devotions.
He insists that the best way of reaching God is to
perform ordinary tasks entirely for the love of God.
When confronted with the challenge to practice
some virtue, Lawrence plainly prayed: "'My God,
I cannot do this unless you enable me to do so' and
he was immediately given the strength needed, and
even more." Conversely, our failure to perceive the
divine presence "restrains the hand of God and
so stops the flow of the abundance of his graces"
which otherwise stream into a faith-filled soul "like
a torrent forcibly diverted from its usual course
which having found a passage pours through ir-
resistibly in an overwhelming flood."

All of this requires constant perseverance, for
"in the spiritual life not to advance is to retreat."
The practice of the presence of God helps fulfill
our end in life: "to become the most perfect adorers of God we possibly can." We worship God in
spirit "by a humble and genuine act of adoration
from the very depths of our soul... as if God were

one with our soul and our soul one with God." We adore God in truth when we "acknowledge that we are completely the opposite to him and that he wishes very much to make us like him if we wish it." Brother Lawrence understands how important it is for us when "we enter upon the spiritual life [that] we should consider in depth who we are." And the principal truth of that self-knowledge is that "the more weak and despicable I see myself to be, the more beloved I am of God. That is how I look upon myself from time to time in this holy presence."

Through our adoration of God in truth we devote ourselves entirely to knowing God: "the more we know him the more we want to know him; the deeper and wider our knowledge, the greater will be our love." In turn, this knowledge compels us to continue to do little things for God "who looks not at the grandeur of these actions but rather at the love with which they are performed." Brother Lawrence reminds us that God's own love for us remains "infinitely more than we imagine." For this reason, the monk's constant desire was "to continue to live only for the love of God," spurred on by the prayer, "Lord, make me according to your heart."

Divine love also disposes us "to receive from God, with equanimity, the sweet and the bitter, and even the most painful and most difficult trials." For if our love of God is authentic and truly great, "we will love him equally in sorrow and in joy." This helps us to comprehend our sinfulness and the right way to respond to it: "Relying on the infinite merits of our Lord, we should, with complete confidence, ask for his grace regardless of our sins." In Brother Lawrence's mind, this is only natural since "the greater perfection a soul aspires to, the more dependent it is upon grace.... If only we knew how we need God's grace, we would never lose sight of him, not even for an instant."

But Brother Lawrence lends us his own example to teach us how to act when we do lose sight of God. In the knowledge of some fault, he prayed to God simply: "I shall never do otherwise if you leave me to myself; it is up to you to keep me from falling and to correct what is wrong." His confidence in God's mercy flows from his knowledge of the history of salvation: "God seemed to choose the greatest sinners, rather than those who had lived in innocence, to bestow his greatest graces on, for by this action was clearly revealed his ineffable goodness." In his prayers, Brother Lawrence envisioned God's reward for such trust in divine mercy: "God sometimes took him by the hand and led him before the entire court of heaven to reveal to all the wretch on whom he so graciously bestowed his graces."

This same confidence informs the way we deal with spiritual aridity "by which God tries our love for him." Brother Lawrence reminds us that

God, in his mysterious Providence, "has several ways of drawing us to him; sometimes he hides himself from us." God can be present under strange guises: "God is often nearer in times of illness and weakness than when we are in a perfect state of health. He sometimes permits the body to suffer to cure the illness of our souls." The mortification of suffering or of self-imposed asceticism only increases our delight in God's presence, for "God does not allow a soul entirely devoted to him to have any other pleasure than with him." Therefore, when human nature contests our spiritual efforts "you must go against your human inclinations. Often you will think you are wasting time, but you must go on."

Our vigilance to God's presence immerses us in God's will so that we "become abandoned to God in the manner he wishes us to." It consoles us with the understanding that "one does not become holy all at once." Devotion to God's presence and his holy will effects a refashioning — a transfiguration — in us: "Sometimes I think of myself as a block of stone before a sculptor, ready to be sculpted into a statue, presenting myself thus to God, and I beg him to form his perfect image in my soul and make me entirely like himself." This conformity to God enlightens us to see that our sanctification consists in "doing for God what we ordinarily do for ourselves." In short, the practice is the kind "submission of the heart and mind to the will of God" that enables authentic devotion and perfection to exist.

In sum, Brother Lawrence counsels: "Think of God often, adore him continually, live and die with him; that is the glorious business of a Christian; in a word, it is our calling." And we must not delay: "Get going on this work; if you do as he wishes, be assured you will soon see the results." For "God has infinite treasures to give us."

12

True Devotion to
the Blessed Virgin Mary

Of all the promoters of Marian spirituality, Pope John Paul II singles out the author of *True Devotion to the Blessed Virgin Mary* in his encyclical on the Blessed Mother, *Redemptoris Mater*: "I would like to recall the figure of Saint Louis-Marie Grignion de Montfort who proposes consecration to Christ through the hands of Mary as an effective means for Christians to live faithfully their baptismal commitments" (48).

The eighteenth-century saint makes clear his purpose. "My aim is to show that Mary has been but very imperfectly known until now, and that this is one of the reasons why Jesus Christ is not known as he deserves to be known. Our aim in establishing solid devotion to the Most Blessed Virgin is none other than to establish more perfectly the worship of Jesus Christ, and to provide an easier and safer way by which we can find Jesus Christ."

In accordance with the desire of divine

Providence, "the Blessed Virgin was necessary to God" in the work of salvation. As a result, Mary "is much more necessary to people if they are to achieve their final end." But de Montfort is not content merely to posit that Mary is vital to our salvation. Rather, he endeavors to show why devotion to the Blessed Mother remains indispensable to the Christian life. In so doing, he seeks to amend the thinking of those who act "as though Marian devotion were merely something optional in our spiritual life."

De Montfort points out three key reasons for practicing devotion to Mary. He begins first of all by voicing a common inquiry: "But are we in need of a mediator with the Mediator himself? Is our purity sufficiently great to warrant our uniting ourselves with him directly and of ourselves?" The author responds that indeed we do require a principle of purification in our lives of faith… and that is Mary. For, because "the world was unworthy to receive the Son of God immediately from the hands of the Father, he gave that Son to Mary in order that the world should receive him through her."

Therefore, Mary's mediatory role consists in making us worthy to receive Jesus her Son. As *True Devotion* teaches: "It is through Mary that we can draw near to God and unite ourselves perfectly and closely to God's divine majesty.… This devotion to the Blessed Virgin is a perfect way to reach Jesus

Christ and to unite ourselves with him."

How does Mary act as a means of purification? "This good Mother purifies all our good works, embellishes them, and causes them to be accepted by her divine Son. When our good works are given into the pure and fruitful hands of Mary, these same hands.... will cleanse that gift of everything that could render it tainted or imperfect."

By relying on the Blessed Mother to purify our prayers and offerings, we comply with God's Providence. As de Montfort instructs us: "The Blessed Virgin is the means used by Christ to come to us; and she is also the means we must use to go to him.... Mary's master purpose is to unite us with Jesus Christ, her Son; and it is the most decided wish of her Son that we should come to him through his Blessed Mother."

At the same time, devotion to Mary counteracts the sin of pride which tempts us to think that, on our own, we can give God the glory he deserves. "This is exactly what we do by our devotion to Mary: we offer and consecrate all that we are and all that we possess to the Blessed Virgin, in order that, through her mediation, Our Lord may receive the glory and the gratitude which we owe him."

In addition to the purity that enables us to enter into a sanctified relationship with God, we require a spiritual conformity in order to sustain that relationship. Mary is crucial also in this regard. De Montfort explains that "only through Mary has the Holy Spirit formed Jesus Christ; and only through her does he form the members of Christ's Mystical Body.... God the Son desires to be formed and, as it were, to be incarnated daily, through his Mother."

This conformity happens mystically. *True Devotion* speaks of the Blessed Mother as "the great and unique mold of God, designed to create living images of God.... Whoever is cast in this divine mold is quickly formed and molded in Jesus Christ, and Jesus Christ in that person. At little cost and in a short time, he will become like unto God, since he has been cast into the mold which has shaped God." By depending on Mary as our means of conformity to Jesus, we are saved from the snares of self-sufficiency. For "the more we are consecrated to Mary, the more perfectly are we united with Jesus Christ."

And lastly, just as Mary is the Mother of the life of Jesus, so too is she the Mother of our spiritual life. We are not self-starters in the life of faith. "It is Mary alone who has found grace before God without the aid of another mere creature. All others who have found grace with God have done so only through her."

Our continued growth in the life of faith remains contingent upon our relationship with the Blessed Mother. De Montfort writes: "I do not believe that any person can achieve intimate union with Our Lord and perfect fidelity to the Holy Spirit unless he has established a very deep union with the Blessed Virgin and a great dependence on her help."

Because of the Blessed Mother's unique relationship with the Holy Spirit, "he has chosen Mary to be the dispensatrix of all that he possesses, so that she distributes to whom she wishes, as she wishes and when she wishes, all his gifts and graces, he himself making no heavenly gift to human beings except by her Virginal hands. This is in accordance with the will of God, who has designed that we should have all things in Mary."

One sure way to deepen our union with the Blessed Mother is through the recitation of the Hail Mary. *True Devotion* explains that "since the salvation of mankind began through the Hail Mary, the salvation of each individual soul is linked up with this prayer.... This same prayer, devoutly said, will cause the word of God to germinate in our souls, and to bear the Fruit of Life, Jesus Christ."

In return, true devotion instills in us a tremendous sense of confidence, for "to be entirely and truly devout towards Mary is an infallible sign of predestination." And that makes us join in the longing of de Montfort: "If only it were known what glory and love You receive in this admirable creature, how different would be the feelings of people towards You and towards her!"

13

JEAN-PIERRE DE CAUSSADE

Abandonment to Divine Providence

This masterpiece of spirituality that has inspired and moved untold thousands was never intended to be published. *Abandonment to Divine Providence* is the amalgamation of the many letters, notes, and conferences written for the Visitation nuns of Nancy, France by Jesuit Father Jean-Pierre de Caussade from 1729 to 1739 when, for much of that time, he served as their spiritual director. Fr. Henri Ramiere, S.J. edited these writings and, in 1861, a hundred years after de Caussade's death, published the text with the title *Abandonment to Divine Providence*.

As the title suggests, de Caussade's treatise emphasizes the act of complete self-surrender to God's will in the fervent living of faith. Why is divine Providence given such primacy in this approach? Because it is the will of God that "confers upon all things the power to implant Jesus Christ in the depths of our hearts." Our devotion to divine Providence disposes us to discover the power of Jesus in our lives. For this reason, de Caussade defines holiness as "complete loyalty to God's will." In this he is promoting, not a slavish adherence to a divine mandate, but rather a filial obedience by which "we shall become one with God."

This loving obedience begins simply by longing for God, for then "we enjoy him and all his gifts, and the fullness of our enjoyment exactly matches the extent of our desire for him." It is best expressed in our reverence of the Holy Name, for "to hallow God's name is to know, to worship and to love his adorable will every moment and all that it does." This instills in us the confidence to find God's will at work "even in complete chaos and disorder" as well as "in the wicked deeds which the arrogant man commits to affront it." The infallible efficacy of divine Providence surpasses all.

The grace-filled response to the working of God's will de Caussade calls "abandonment": "a blending of faith, hope, and love in one single act which unites us to God and all his activities" by letting "God act and do all he wishes according to our state in life." In the course of such abandonment, the soul never thinks of itself, but rather remains continually occupied with loving and obeying God: "It relies no longer on its own ideas to help it bear the weariness and difficulties of the journey. It carries on with a profound conviction of its own weakness."

De Caussade describes self-abandonment

as "the normal means of securing special virtues." Therefore, it is *de rigueur* for anyone desiring to live in God "to take care to employ every possible means to achieve a complete surrender to him." The first step to self-abandonment is right self-knowledge by which the soul, "convinced of its own nothingness and certain, too, that all it can derive from itself is harmful, abandons itself to God so that it can have only him and receive all things through him." This humility enlightens us: "Let us acknowledge that we are incapable of becoming holy by our own efforts, and put our trust in God, who would not have taken away our ability to walk unless he was to carry us in his arms."

The divine embrace of abandonment frees us from fears, empties our souls "of all false confidence in our own ability," and spurs us to "leap over the maze of self-love instead of trying to explore its endless alleys." The self-abandoned soul loves all that God does and finds his activity always sanctifying. For abandonment transforms our affections, our appetites, and our desires: "Abandoned souls cannot, as others do, become attached to people or concern themselves with normal aspirations, normal pursuits and activities. They have a conception of sanctity which never ceases to torment them. They can find no pleasure or satisfaction in anything, but must give all their affection to God. He deliberately leads them along this path so that he alone can delight them."

Abandonment illumines our sight as it transforms our heart. Apart from the action of grace, the abandoned soul "sees nothing clearly except those slight defects which grace can turn to good." For the self-abandoned soul "sees only God and its duty." It is blessed with a profound perception of the value of things often overlooked: "Self-abandoned souls always carefully gather up the crumbs which the proud tread underfoot, for everything is precious to them and there is nothing which does not enrich them. They are completely indifferent to everything, yet neglect nothing, for they respect all things and extract from them all that is useful."

Self-surrender to God becomes in turn the means of personal self-fulfillment: "If we all were faithful to grace and responded to it according to our abilities, we should all be satisfied, because we should reach a measure of excellence and place in God's favor that would completely satisfy our desires. We should be well content, according to nature and according to grace." And this perfection in us becomes readily evident to others: "For those who have surrendered themselves completely to God, all they are and do has power. Their lives are sermons. They are apostles. God gives a special force to all they say and do, even to their silence, their tranquillity and their detachment, which, quite unknown to them, profoundly influences other people." The matrix in which we surrender ourselves to the promptings of divine Providence is what de Caussade calls "the sacrament of the present moment."

"Every moment we live through is like an ambassador who declares the will of God." Each moment possesses an integrity and infallibility in the way it furthers our relationship with God. Our attention to the present moment helps us to see how "everything has something divine about it that can lead us onward to holiness. Everything is part of that completeness which is Jesus Christ." This gives us the confidence to believe that "we can find all that is necessary in the present moment. … At every moment God's will produces what is needful for the task at hand, and the simple soul wants neither more nor less than what it has." De Caussade's conviction insists that "what God arranged for us to experience at each moment is the best and holiest thing that could happen to us."

Therefore, since making use of whatever God offers us is the only way of belonging to God, it is incumbent upon every abandoned soul to "seize what each moment brings and then forget it, eager only to be alert to respond to God and live for him alone." This is what the author means when he writes that "each moment brings a duty which must be faithfully fulfilled." This sense of obligation is heightened by the aspect of urgency with which de Caussade regards the present moment: "There is nothing better for us than to do what God wants at any particular moment. We must regard everything else with complete indifference and as something worth nothing at all."

Each individual encounters the present moment in a unique and personal way: "The soul wants to know only what every moment says to it and does not ask what has been said to others. It is fully satisfied with what itself receives, and so, quite unconsciously it grows constantly nearer to God.... There is not a single soul which is not given the divine imprint in a way which best suits its own individuality.... In the world of grace, each one of us has a special grace." As a result, our perfect submission to God's will moment by moment educates and illumines us: "It is what happens moment by moment which enlightens us and gives us that practical knowledge which Jesus Christ himself chose to acquire before beginning his public life." Even more than that, our belief in the efficacy of the present moment opens up to us the most intimate knowledge of God himself: "The realization that God is active in all that happens at every moment is the deepest knowledge we can have in this life of the things of God." This knowledge in turn transforms us: "When God gives himself thus, the commonplace becomes extraordinary. It is a miracle and constant delight; yet, in itself, it has nothing about it to dazzle our senses, but it does turn all the ordinary affairs of life into things which are rare and wonderful."

Our self-abandonment to divine Providence in the present moment quickens in us the life of faith. Faith, as the "mother of tenderness, trust, and joy," prepares us for the truth that "God disguises himself so that we may reach that pure faith which enables us to recognize him under any appearance." Ironically, we recognize the efficacy of God's disguise if we ourselves remain hidden in him nurturing the mustard seed of faith: "You make a root below the soil flourish and you can make fruitful the darkness in which you keep me. So my soul, like a tiny root, will stay hidden in you and your power will make it send forth branches, leaves, blossoms and fruit which, though invisible to you, will nourish and delight the souls of others."

To live by faith, then, means "to live joyfully, to live with assurance, untroubled by doubts and with complete confidence in all we have to do and suffer at each moment by the will of God." The rewards of such abandonment are manifold. "Faith transforms the earth into paradise. The hollowness of all created things is disclosed by faith and it is by faith that God makes his presence plain everywhere. Faith tears aside the veil so that we can see the everlasting truth.... There is no peace more wonderful than the peace we enjoy when faith shows us God in all created things."

In addition, this faith "produces a certain detachment of soul which enables us to handle any situation and every kind of person." It purifies us of self-conceived ideas and high-flown imaginings of God by persuading us that "all you suffer, all you do, all your inclinations are mysteries under which God gives himself to you." We need such faith in order to see God at work in "the raging torrent of so much distress, so many troubles, so much embarrassment and weakness, and so many setbacks" that he allows. In turn, faith, de Caussade assures us, "is nourished and strengthened by these happenings."

Faith, then, constantly reminds us that "ours is not a life governed by our feelings." Rather, "we must keep ourselves detached from all we feel or do if we are to travel along his path and live only for God and the duties of the present moment." As a result, "perfection is presented to the soul contrary to all its preconceived ideas, to all that it feels and to all that it has learned. It now comes to the soul in the form of all the afflictions sent by Providence." By faith we recognize that trials are sent "so that our lives may be made more splendid by our overcoming them." When we feel baffled by our weakness, "it is at this moment that God appears in all his glory to those who belong wholly to him and disentangles them from all their troubles far more easily than novelists." This process sanctifies us, for "holiness means the eager acceptance of every trial sent by God" since behind every trial "God is acting and giving us something of the divine which will give us the brilliance of the sun."

Faith teaches us that "God takes away everything from us if we give ourselves entirely to him." In fact, de Caussade goes so far as to assert that "in this state of self-abandonment, everything that happens to our soul and body has the aspect of death." And yet, "when God takes from us the things we can see and understand, he always returns them under another form" since "the spirit which makes us suffer is the only one which can comfort us." He comforts us by means of unmitigated generosity: "Where God is concerned, the more we seem to lose, the more we gain; the more he strips us of natural things, the more he showers us with supernatural gifts."

Therefore, if our attempt to live by faith fills us with feelings of desolation, God gives us "an inner assurance that we need be afraid of nothing as long as we allow him to act and abandon ourselves to him." The author understands that "there is nothing more distressing for a soul that wants to do only the will of God and yet cannot feel certain that it loves him." That is why at times "the divine will withdraws itself from view and stands behind the soul to push it forward," for "nothing stimulates the desire for union with the divine will so powerfully as this apparent loss."

Love is what it is all about, for "our holiness is measured by our love of God, and it increases in proportion to the growth of our desire to obey his will and his plans for us, no matter what they are." We rely on the trials of the world because "we cannot be settled in the state of pure love until we have experienced a lot of setbacks and many humiliations." Jesus' love, in an attempt to unite itself with us through all the world contains, "uses both the best and worst of his creatures." We surrender ourselves to his divine purpose because "the whole business of self-abandonment is only the business of loving, and love achieves everything."

In the end, self-abandonment to divine Providence teaches us that "there can be nothing great in us — with one exception: our total receptivity to God's will." And yet, that receptivity makes us saints, and "the life of each saint is the life of Jesus Christ. It is a new Gospel." That is why "our life here is a spectacle which makes heaven rejoice."

14

Story of a Soul

Master storyteller Garrison Keillor describes the grade-school heroine of one of his tales in this way: "She was amazing and wonderful because God loved her, and she took that love so that things which were common and ordinary became graceful and elegant." He could very well have been describing St. Therese of Lisieux of the Child Jesus and the Holy Face. Popularly known as the "Little Flower," Therese was a French Carmelite nun who died of tuberculosis in 1897 at the age of twenty-four.

Under obedience to religious superiors, Therese composed her autobiography entitled *Story of a Soul*. The book is a masterpiece of memory that skillfully integrates every significant event from childhood on that contributed to the fruition of her Carmelite vocation.

Unfortunately, too many tend to bypass the work, misjudging its relevance. The reader must understand how the saint's reminiscences were naturally conditioned by nineteenth-century French cultural sensibilities. The frame of reference for Therese's experiences is an urbane, well-to-do family in which proper etiquette was cultivated and Catholic faith fervently embraced. The family favored demonstrative shows of affection and an overt mode of piety.

Therefore, it would be a mistake to critique or dismiss *Story of a Soul* on the basis of its decorous literary style and obsolete social propriety. Instead, the best way to read St. Therese is with penetrating sensitivity to her magnificent powers of observation and recollection. It is astounding what she remembers and how she interprets those memories.

For Therese is a master of analogy. She is able to intuit the divine significance of common and mundane happenings... to make connections between the trivial and the transcendent. Those who pooh-pooh the writing of St. Therese violate the heart of her profound doctrine whose genius consists in championing the truth that, in God's Providence, nothing is trivial.

In promoting her "Little Way," Therese insists upon harnessing the seemingly insignificant moments of life as crucial tools for demonstrating love. "I have no other means of proving my love for you, God, than that of... not allowing one little sacrifice to escape, not one look, one word, profiting by all the smallest things and doing them through love."

This spiritual strategy manifests, not an unreflective naïveté, but rather a tenacious courageousness. For Therese's doctrine, like her book, is the fruit of a childhood brimming with sorrow, suffering, and separation. She recounts the heart-rending and graphic memory — at age four — of kissing the corpse of her mother on the day of her death from cancer. Similarly, by the time she received the Carmelite habit, as a girl of sixteen, her father had succumbed to a severely disabling mental illness. This prompted Therese to write: "On the day of my wedding I was really an orphan, no longer having a Father on this earth."

In recalling such distressing memories, Therese admits with cryptic foreboding: "I saw many things they would have hidden from me." One might think that Therese should prefer to hide these things from us so as to spare herself any added grief. On the contrary, the saint deliberately employs these agonizing experiences in constructing the paradigm for her spiritual doctrine. In this we witness the scope of her fortitude.

For Therese's Little Way is the way of spiritual childhood, "the way of trust and absolute surrender." Therese discovered the path to perfection within the miseries of her girlhood. Therefore, she proposes to perpetuate the dynamics of that childhood in the pursuit of sanctity.

In so doing, Therese provides an alternative to the complex and complicated programs of spiritual growth prevalent in her day. "I want to seek out a means of going to heaven by a little way, a way that is very straight, very short, and totally new." She uses the image of a (then) new invention to express her spiritual intention: "I wanted to find an elevator which would raise me to Jesus, for I am too small to climb the rough stairway of perfection.... The elevator which must raise me to heaven is your arms, O Jesus! And for this... I had to remain little and become this more and more."

Therese's doctrine of the Little Way recognizes that "Jesus finds few hearts who surrender to him without reservations, who understand the real tenderness of his infinite love." Once we recognize our own negligence in these two areas of humility and charity, the teaching of St. Therese ably propels our growth in holiness.

The Little Way demands that we honestly accept the fact of our own littleness, as Therese herself did unceasingly throughout her life. "There is always present to my mind the remembrance of what I am.... I am not disturbed at seeing myself weakness itself. On the contrary, it is in my weakness that I glory, and I expect each day to discover new imperfections in myself."

Humility such as this purifies us of any false claims to God's favor: "The soul knows that nothing in herself was capable of attracting the divine glances, and his mercy alone brought about everything that is good in her.... It is only love which makes us acceptable to God." In fact, as Therese's own life testifies, this powerlessness itself emboldens the believer: "It is my weakness that gives me the boldness of offering myself as victim of your love, O Jesus."

According to the saint, true humility is characterized by a confidence that expresses itself in abandonment: "I feel that if you found a soul weaker and littler than mine, which is impossible, you would be pleased to grant it still greater favors, provided it abandoned itself with total confidence to your infinite mercy." Ultimately, this childlike dependence is a cause, not for despair, but for joy: "I am simply resigned to see myself always imperfect and in this I find my joy."

"My own folly," writes Therese, "is this: to trust that your love will accept me." This exchange of love is also crucial to the Little Way. But Therese's doctrine requires a particular kind of loving. "It is no longer a question of loving one's neighbor as oneself but of loving him as he, Jesus, has loved him, and will love him to the consummation of the ages."

As a result, the Little Way impels us to relinquish our own concepts and management of love. Therese confesses: "You know very well that never would I be able to love my sisters as you love them unless you, O Jesus, loved them in me.... Yes, I feel it, when I am charitable, it is Jesus alone who is acting in me, and the more united I am to him, the more also do I love my sisters."

In the end, "perfection consists in doing God's will, in being what he wills us to be." The spiritual teaching of St. Therese of Lisieux, like her life, can be summarized in the final two words of her autobiography: "confidence and love." Those who need more of either should turn to her book.

The Pattern of Holiness

In order to recapitulate the major insights of the great spiritual masters, we do well to examine what it is about their teaching that makes it expressly Catholic. For as we concentrate on the Catholic essence of these works, we readily discover the common ideas the writers share, especially by means of seven prominent, recurrent themes. We discover as well the principle that unites them over a span of fifteen centuries. And we connect with the dynamic that makes each of these works a classic.

Belief in God's Love

All of the classic Catholic authors agree that the foundation of the whole life of faith is an ardent belief in and acceptance of God's love. That is to say, the point of departure in the spiritual life is a heartfelt approach to the reality of God's love in the way that he wills to give it. Our reluctance to embody God's authentic love remains the cause of much spiritual sorrow and inertia. As St. Therese of Lisieux profoundly points out, "Jesus finds few hearts who surrender to him without reservation, who understand the real tenderness of his infinite love."

The question is: Why? Why are we so grudging in giving ourselves to God? And why are we suspicious and ignorant of the tenderness of God's unbounded love? The answer is that we lack the essential self-knowledge that renders a right and authentic conception of ourselves. For, in God's Providence, the only truthful way that we can understand ourselves, our purpose, and our ultimate dignity is from within the embrace of God's love. Julian of Norwich shows us the reality of this when she writes: "Before God made us he loved us. We are made for love, in which love God endlessly protects us." St. Francis de Sales explains how God's intention to love us penetrates and eviscerates even the evil of human sin: "On the tree of the Cross, the Heart of Jesus beheld your heart and loved it."

God makes this same declaration to St. Catherine of Siena: "Without having been loved by you, I loved you unspeakably much." St. Catherine's response represents the fundamental disposition required of everyone beginning the life of faith: "With unimaginable love you looked upon your creatures within your very self, and you fell in love with us. So it was love that made you create us and give us being just so that we might taste your supreme and eternal good." We are commanded to believe the truth that God takes the initiative in loving us, that love is his motive in creating us, that God chooses us in love because of his goodness, that human evil cannot impede the constant offering of divine love, and that we find our personal fulfillment in the loving response we make in turn to God's love.

Therefore, only when we take possession of divine love do we gain that self-possession which radically promotes our life. Refusal to accede to the truth of God's love leaves us unsatisfied and incomplete, as St. Augustine reminds us in his lament: "O Lord, you have made us for yourself, and our heart is restless until it rests in you."

The certitude of God's love remains amply proven in the graciousness of creation. St. Francis of Assisi confirms this truth in his sermon to the birds: "The creator loves you very much since he gives you so many good things." Julian of Norwich expresses the same insight in this way: "It is God's will that I see myself bound to him in love as if everything he had done, he had done for me." Along with God's good gifts, then, the Lord insists that we make his very love our own, and to do so with the same love that he loves us.

Again, St. Therese of Lisieux comes to our

assistance in grasping this mystery: "For me to love you, Jesus, as you love me, I would have to borrow your own love and then only would I be at rest." The Lord delights in making such a permanent loan to us. In fact, he commands us to love him in this manner, as St. Catherine relates: "I ask you to love me with the same love with which I love you." This true love of God is St. Francis de Sales' ultimate definition of "devotion."

Of course, we are the ones who benefit in several ways from loving God back with the same love with which he loves us. Such love enlightens our knowledge of ourselves and of God, as Thomas à Kempis notes: "By truly loving you I have found myself and you." This love is the source of our every accomplishment and the standard of our sanctity, as Jean-Pierre de Caussade makes clear: "The whole business of self-abandonment is only the business of loving, and love achieves everything…. Our holiness is measured by our love of God."

However, not only our holiness, but the merit of every undertaking is determined by the quality of divine love that informs it. Several of the authors forcefully make this point. St. John of the Cross writes: "The value of Christian good works is not based upon their quantity and quality so much as upon the love of God practiced in them." So, too, St. Teresa of Avila: "The Lord does not care so much for the importance of our works as for the love with which they are done." Brother Lawrence of the Resurrection also echoes this: "God looks not at the grandeur of our actions but rather at the love with which they are performed." In fact, this essential theme resounds in the teaching of all Christian spiritual masters.

Just as divine love gives authentic meaning and value to any action, so too does it illumine the end and goal of our lives. Brother Lawrence always strove "to make the love of God the end of all his actions." St. Ignatius of Loyola testified to the all-encompassing integrity of God's love when he prayed: "Give me love of yourself, Lord, along with your grace, for that is enough for me."

Only such love defeats the downward tug of human nature toward selfishness and sensuality. It elevates our affections, enabling us to love God for who he is, instead of for what he does. For, as the author of *The Cloud of Unknowing* observes, "it is far better to love and praise God for what he is in himself, desiring him for his own sake."

Since our own self-conception becomes mired by our misunderstanding of the tenderness of the Lord's infinite love, God gives us Mary, the Immaculate Conception, to assist us in loving God the way he deserves. St. Louis de Montfort writes: "This Mother of fair love will open your heart and make it big and generous. As a result, you will be led by pure love of him who is love. You will look upon him as your own good Father.... Devotion to the Blessed Virgin is a perfect way to reach Jesus

Christ and to unite ourselves with him."

Then, as St. Therese notes, "it is no longer a question of loving one's neighbor as oneself but of loving him as he, Jesus, has loved him." In the wonder of that love we experience the beatitude for which we were made: "Blessed is he who appreciates what it is to love Jesus" (Thomas à Kempis).

God's Mercy, Sin, and the Mode of the Soul

The radical acceptance of the reality of God's love delves us more deeply into the mystery of the way God cares for us. In particular, it opens us up to the power of God's mercy, and enables us to comprehend the providential role of sin in the Christian's life. At times, divine Providence seems paradoxical, for as Julian of Norwich teaches, "sin is necessary, but all will be well, and all will be well, and every kind of thing will be well." St. Francis de Sales observes that "we can never be completely free of venial sins, yet we can avoid all affection for venial sins."

However, this circumstance must not prompt us to despair, for by our healthy sense of sin we appropriate the saving richness of God's mercy. Julian of Norwich writes: "We need to fall to know how feeble and wretched we are in ourselves, and to know the wonderful love of our creator." This, then, is the twofold purpose of sin in God's Providence: to endow us with unerring self-knowledge, and to bless us with a grace-filled conviction about God's mercy. The two are inseparable. For this reason, St. Catherine of Siena relates the Lord's command: "I do not want the soul to think about her sins without calling to mind the greatness of my mercy." As *The Little Flowers of St. Francis* puts it: "You must always believe that God's power to forgive is greater than your power to sin."

At the same time, it is a good, and holy, and necessary thing to reflect on our sinfulness. *The Cloud of Unknowing* teaches that the Christian cannot begin contemplation "until one has first purified his conscience of all particular sins." St. Ignatius of Loyola stresses the importance of such self-examination when he directs his retreatants to begin the first week of the spiritual exercises by reflecting on personal sinfulness. It is as important for our spiritual life as it is for our eternal life, as St. Teresa of Avila reminds us: "It would be madness to think we could get to heaven without sometimes retiring into our souls so as to know ourselves, or thinking of our failings and of what we owe to God, or frequently imploring his mercy."

Such recollection purifies the soul, as St. Augustine assures in stating the purpose of his *Confessions*: "I will now call to mind my past foulness and the abominable things I did in those days... The memory is bitter, but by it you grow sweet unto me, Lord." And we never go without the need to do this, for, as St. Teresa of Avila notes, "sorrow for sin increases in proportion to the divine grace received."

This mindfulness of our weakness fills us with a holy humility that, ironically, makes us unsurpassably strong. Thomas à Kempis writes: "Left to myself, I am nothing but total weakness. But if you look upon me I am at once made strong." Belief in this truth leads St. Therese of Lisieux to assert: "I am simply resigned to see myself always imperfect and in this I find my joy." Such realistic assessment of self enables us to recognize the Providence of God at work even in evil. As de Caussade points out, "an abandoned soul carries on with a profound conviction of its own weakness.... It respects God's working even in the wicked deeds which the arrogant man commits to affront it."

Therefore, it is the hallmark of Christian greatness for one confidently to acknowledge personal imperfection within the context of divine mercy. As *Little Flowers* declares: "Blessed is he who always has his sin and the goodness of God before his eyes, for he can look forward to a great consolation." This consolation remains the fruit of divine compassion, as St. Therese professes: "God's mercy alone brought about everything that is good in us." This mercy is demonstrated most poignantly in the way God elects to favor the least deserving. Brother Lawrence understood this: "God seemed to choose the greatest sinners to bestow his graces on, for by this action was clearly revealed his ineffable goodness."

Authentic mercy draws us into deeper communion with the Church and the saints. St. Louis de Montfort cautions: "Let no one claim that he has received God's mercy if he offends his Blessed Mother." Therefore, we are asked to accept our divinely-ordained struggle with human weakness as the means God chooses to unleash his mercy and to unite all together in love. It is the means best suited to the needs of our human nature. For God's tenderness informs every moment of our growth, all the while prospering grace to build on human nature. As St. John of the Cross confirms: "In order that God lift the soul from the extreme of its low state to the other state of divine union, he must do so with order, gently, and according to the mode of the soul."

The Instrumentality of the Church and the Communion of Saints

Continued growth in God's love and the benefits of divine mercy requires the Christian's participation in and reliance on the Body of Christ. Holiness does not happen in a vacuum. It is learned via the influence of holy exemplars. Sanctity comes by association with the saints. The

Catholic spiritual masters emphasize the role of the Church and the mediation of the elect as integral to Christian perfection. The Lord says to St. Catherine of Siena: "I wanted to make you dependent on one another so that each of you would be my minister dispensing the graces you have received from me."

This mutual ecclesial dependence manifests the beauty and goodness of God's Providence. It liberates us from the evils of self-sufficiency and pride, it urges us to anticipate the needs of others and to respond to them with divine generosity, it endows us with magnificent graces we could not grasp on our own, it saves us from isolation and alienation by uniting us together, it demonstrates our indispensability to the Body of Christ, and it keeps us constantly and reverently thankful. Moreover, such receptivity to the exigencies of the Church is itself redemptive, as an angel promises in the case of St. Francis of Assisi: "No one, no matter how great a sinner he is, will fail to obtain mercy from God if he has a heartfelt love for your Order."

For this reason, Julian of Norwich directs that her book be read only by "those who will submit themselves to the faith of Holy Church." Such submission assures our union with the Holy Spirit, for, as St. Ignatius of Loyola observes, "the same Spirit guides and governs Holy Mother Church."

St. Teresa of Avila asserts: "It is of the utmost

importance for a person to associate with those who lead a spiritual life." St. Therese of Lisieux takes up this same theme when she writes: "Children learn the sublime song of divine love from souls responsible for forming them." The Church, as Holy Mother, remains the principal formator of God's children. The dynamic of this formation is revealed in the life of Mary, the Model of the Church. St. Louis de Montfort writes: "This good Mother purifies all our good works, embellishes them, and causes them to be accepted by her divine Son."

This truth is played out in a preeminent manner in the conversion of St. Augustine. Augustine came to faith as a result of his prolonged exposure to the life of the Church: the intercessory prayer of his mother Monica, the preaching of St. Ambrose, the actualization of Sacred Scripture, the enticement of the communion of saints, etc. St. Augustine includes in the *Confessions* his mother's last request before dying: "It does not matter where you bury my body. This only I ask: that you would remember me at the Lord's altar, wherever you may be." In this way, St. Augustine attests to the paramount priority of the Church.

God seeks to bestow greater evangelical power on us through the efficacy of the Church. St. John of the Cross expresses this: "To declare and strengthen truth on the basis of natural reason, God draws near those who come together in an endeavor to know it." In this way, the life of the Church unites us more deeply to the life of the three Persons of the Blessed Trinity.

St. Francis de Sales reinforces the import of the corporate actions of the Church when he counsels: "There is always more benefit to be derived from the public offices of the Church than from private particular acts." However, as individual Christians we continue to make our own unique contribution to the upbuilding of the People of God. *The Cloud of Unknowing* observes that when a person has a reputation for outstanding prayerfulness, "good people are honored and delighted to be in his company, strengthened by the sense of God he radiates." Even private devotion becomes elevated and transformed to serve the Church. "Those who have surrendered themselves completely to God are apostles," writes Jean-Pierre de Caussade. "God gives a special force to all they say and do which profoundly influences other people."

We may not even be aware of how God uses our faith as an instrument of grace for others. As St. John of the Cross reminds us, "at times God will give the soul a desire to pray for others whom it has never known nor heard of." Moreover, it was such confidence in the power of divine Providence to perfect personal virtue while enriching the good of the Church that led St. Therese of Lisieux to declare: "Yes, I have found my place in the Church and it is you, O my God, who have given me this place; in the heart of the Church, my Mother, I shall be Love. "

This relationship of love is not limited to our time on earth. It extends into eternal life in the communion of the saints. The saints' love of God continues to affect and inform our own relationship with him. St. Therese of Lisieux confessed: "I felt there was a heaven peopled with souls who actually love me, who consider me their child." Through our life in the Church we appreciate more fervently the privilege of being claimed by God's love. Brother Lawrence recounts that "God sometimes took him by the hand and led him before the entire court of heaven to reveal to all the wretch on whom he had so graciously bestowed his graces." Such a display does not prompt jealousy in the saints, but rather delight, for, as Julian of Norwich acknowledges, the holy ones on earth become "endless marvelous bliss to all who are in heaven."

Thomas à Kempis speaks for all the spiritual masters in commending the saints to us: "Their power to stimulate us to perfection ought to be greater than that of the lukewarm to tempt us to laxity." The unique and supreme role in this regard of the Blessed Mother, the Queen of the Saints, is made clear by St. Louis de Montfort: "All others who have found grace with God have done so only through Mary."

The Importance of Prayer and Struggles with Aridity

Why do all the Catholic spiritual masters insist on the importance of prayer for maturity in the faith? St. Therese of Lisieux sums it up when she says: "It is prayer, it is sacrifice which gives me all my strength; these are the invincible weapons which Jesus has given me." As the author of *The Cloud of Unknowing* reminds us: "By love God may be touched and embraced, never by thought." Prayer is the act of love that serves as the means of uniting ourselves to God. St. Teresa of Avila concurs when she says that through prayer "the will becomes united in some way with the will of God."

Prayer remains essential to the life of faith as a remedy to the ills of the world. St. Catherine of Siena explains that "the medicine by which God wills to heal the whole world is humble, constant, holy prayer." St. Augustine personally experienced the reparative effects of unceasing intercessory prayer offered by his mother Monica for his conversion.

This entree to the life of grace is itself the effect of grace. *The Little Flowers of St. Francis* reminds us that "it is no small thing to be given the grace of holy prayer."

And yet, prayer is not always easy. St. Therese of Lisieux admits that "prayer is a cry of gratitude and love in the midst of trial as well as joy." She recalls a time in her life when "absolute aridity and almost total abandonment were my lot."

Serious struggles with spiritual aridity distinguish the lives of the greatest saints. The challenge is to understand the role aridity plays in God's Providence, and to know how to respond to it.

The Lord explains the meaning of spiritual aridity from within the context of humility and charity to St. Catherine of Siena: "I withdraw from them to humble them and to make them know my charity toward them when they find it in the good will I support in them in time of conflict." De Caussade further develops this same insight by emphasizing the spiritual advantage of aridity: "The divine will withdraws itself from view and stands behind the soul to push it forward. Nothing stimulates the desire for union with the divine will so powerfully as this apparent loss."

St. Ignatius of Loyola insists that aridity is necessary in order "to test how far we will extend ourselves in the service of God." Without that challenge of aridity, we might never be certain. Aridity, then, strengthens and advances our prudence and fortitude. St. Teresa of Avila recognizes this: "Bad thoughts and aridities are often permitted by God to assail and torment us... to teach us to be more on our guard in the future." This is the truest definition of what it means to live by faith, as St. John of the Cross explains: "A soul must advance to union with God's wisdom by unknowing... by blinding itself and remaining in darkness."

Once we understand the divine purpose

for aridity, the spiritual masters also help us understand how to deal with it. St. Francis de Sales suggests that the first thing to do is not to wish it away: "There is nothing so profitable and fruitful in states of aridity as not to have too much longing for release from them." Instead, as St. John of the Cross counsels, "the soul should learn to remain in God's presence with a loving attention and tranquil intellect, even though he seems to himself to be idle."

The aridity that deprives us of comforting feeling also impels us to reach out to God in faith. Julian of Norwich asserts: "The more abased we are, the more profitable it is for us to touch God. He wants us promptly to attend to the touching of his grace." Thomas à Kempis advises us to direct our touch to the wounds of Jesus: "If you turn devoutly to the wounds and precious stigmata of Christ, you will find great comfort in suffering."

Our struggles with prayer prepare us to deal with our struggles with life. As a result, every moment of the day should be lived prayerfully as a way of constantly worshipping God in all we do. Brother Lawrence of the Resurrection reminds us that time set aside for prayer is no different from other times: "We are equally obliged to God by work in the time assigned to work as by prayer during prayer time."

In all of our prayers and in our struggles with aridity, we are never alone. St. Louis de Montfort reminds us that "God has chosen Mary to be the dispensatrix of all that he possesses.... God deigned that we should have all things in Mary." This divine solicitude encourages us and further compels us to attain the ultimate goal of human life which, in the words of Brother Lawrence, is "to become the most perfect adorers of God we possibly can."

The Dynamic of Detachment and Holy Indifference

Once the soul experiences some measure of maturity in the life of faith, the need for detachment and holy indifference becomes urgent. Each of the spiritual masters emphasizes this reality in his or her own way. Julian of Norwich articulates the anthropological rationale for cultivating detachment: "Our soul may never have rest in anything which is beneath itself." St. Augustine takes this position one step further: "If a soul clings to things whose beauty lies outside God, it is riveted only upon sorrow." Detachment, then, enables our self-fulfillment by liberating us from false attachments that threaten to constrain our freedom and diminish our dignity.

Holy indifference to created things remains crucial for continued growth in grace. For this reason, Julian of Norwich counsels us to regard "as nothing all things which are created." Thomas à Kempis recognizes the commitment to indifference as an essential turning point in our relationship with God: "When a man reaches a point where he seeks no solace from any creature, then he begins to relish God perfectly." The author of *The Cloud* expresses this insight from the point of view of prayer: "The very heart of contemplative prayer is nothing but a naked intent toward God for his own sake."

Along with these exalted ends, detachment also serves some rather mundane ones. As St. Francis de Sales reminds us: "With the single exception of sin, anxiety is the greatest evil that can happen to a soul." Holy indifference preserves us from the evil of anxiety by keeping our priorities secure in the things of God. In the process, it purifies our heart of what can harm it most. Thomas à Kempis writes: "Nothing so mars and defiles the heart of man as impure attachment to created things." The impure attachments of the heart invariably infect the flesh, which leads *The Little Flowers of St. Francis* to warn us: "It is impossible for a man to attain to grace unless he gives up sensuality."

In short, detachment and indifference are effective means of putting our confidence in the care of divine Providence. De Caussade expresses his own conviction about this: "There is nothing better for us than to do what God wants at any particular moment. We must regard everything else with complete indifference and as something worth nothing at all." Such detachment invests us with unfailing trust in the will of God while it instills in us a sure sense about what we should value in life.

The price of such detachment is a willingness to go without the comforts and gratifications we might otherwise crave. That is to say, holy indifference endows us with the kind of poverty that, *Little Flowers* tells us, "accompanied Christ on the cross and was buried with him in the tomb." And yet, our love for God's compassionate will only increases our zeal to be utterly detached. This is why St. John of the Cross encourages the Christian to "labor to divest and deprive oneself for God of all that is not God."

Holy indifference blesses us with singleness of purpose and purity of heart. St. Teresa of Avila observes: "The important thing is to love much and to love God without any motive of self-interest." For our utter self-donation and childlike dependence on God augment our authentic appreciation of God's goodness. St. Teresa continues: "The soul neither knows nor desires anything save that God shall do with it what he wills." This heartfelt confidence in divine Providence fired the prayer of St. Ignatius of Loyola, which serves as a fitting model for true Christian detachment: "Take, Lord, receive all I have and possess."

The dynamic of detachment and holy indifference was embodied in a perfect manner in the life of the Blessed Mother. St. Louis de Montfort writes: "Mary neither desires nor does anything which is contrary to the eternal and immutable will of God." Therefore, he encourages us to deepen our union with Mary so that we might share her devotion to the will of God. And we should do so lavishly, without fear: "Attachment to other creatures can have the effect of estranging us from God, but it is not so with our attachment to Mary."

True detachment means possessing a rectified indifference to material things, to our felt desires, and even to our long-held ideas and conceptions. St. Therese of Lisieux links this understanding of detachment to perfection. "Perfection consists in doing God's will, in being what he wills us to be.... Jesus does not demand great actions from us but simply surrender and gratitude." As Brother Lawrence of the Resurrection concludes: "We should surrender ourselves entirely and with complete abandonment to God and take our happiness in doing as he wills." God's words to St. Catherine of Siena are meant for us as well if we want to grow in faith: "Fall in love with my Providence!"

The Redemptive Role of Suffering

As we ponder the wonder of Revelation — God's love, his mercy, the Church — one mysterious question recurs: Why is suffering part of God's plan? St. Augustine wrestled with this enigma which led him to write: "I sought to find where evil comes from, and there was no solution." The excruciating ordeal of suffering that St. John of the Cross himself personally experienced just prior to writing *The Ascent of Mount Carmel* receives no direct reference in his book. Rather, the saint regards his suffering with docility and resolution as something fitting and helpful toward his own sanctification.

Thomas à Kempis tells us that "suffering is the way to the kingdom of heaven." And with this all the Catholic spiritual masters concur. Thomas à Kempis goes on: "It is better for you to be tried in adversities than to have all things as you wish." As Jean-Pierre de Caussade relates, suffering provides the proper disposition for holiness: "We cannot be settled in the state of pure love until we have experienced a lot of setbacks and many humiliations." *The Little Flowers of St. Francis* voices this same theme: "No one should consider himself a perfect friend of God until he has passed through many temptations."

In particular, suffering enables us to go beyond the distress of the world in embracing the transcendent. The author of *The Cloud of Unknowing* writes: "Both sinners and innocents will suffer in the work of contemplation to win that personal wholeness beyond all pain." Furthermore, suffering, in the assessment of St. Francis de Sales, remains a sign of divine favor and election: "God permits violent assaults only in souls whom he desires to raise up to his own pure and surpassing love."

Our struggle with external, earthly pain leads us to see the source of real evil within. St. John of the Cross writes: "The soul's greatest suffering is caused by the knowledge of its own miseries. It is a time to give comfort and encouragement that they may desire to endure this suffering as long as God wills." This common experience with suffering serves as an effective instrument of communion and compassion. St. Therese of Lisieux shares her discovery of this insight: "Jesus made me understand that it was through suffering that he wanted to give me souls, and my attraction for suffering grew in proportion to its increase." Therefore, the deepest suffering which is a sign of our need for grace remains destined in turn to become a source of grace for others.

The authors note several positive effects of suffering in the life of faith. St. Francis expresses the compassion of God to one of his friars afflicted with moral trials when he says: "I love you more the more you are attacked by temptations." For suffering makes us more receptive to God's mercy. It rids us of deceptive self-reliance, and opens up to us new reserves of spiritual strength and resilience. It reveals the power of God's love as it enables us at the same time to appropriate divine love and to share it with others. This truth prompts St. Catherine of Siena to boast that "suffering and sorrow increase in proportion to love." St. Ignatius of Loyola stresses the importance of this dynamic in making an intense meditation on the suffering and Passion of Christ a major component of his *Spiritual Exercises.*

Therefore, suffering in the Christian perspective is not a sign of rejection, but rather of divine election. Julian of Norwich remarks: "God wishes us to know that he keeps us safe all the time, in joy and in sorrow, and that he loves us as much in sorrow as in joy." Only a humble spirit frees us enough to accept this truth, and even in this suffering assists us. St. Teresa of Avila refers to suffering as "a great mercy on the part of God through which we gain a great deal of humility."

The great paradox of suffering for Christ is the inestimable way it fortifies us. *Little Flowers* asserts: "If the Lord should make stones and rocks rain from heaven, they would not hurt us if we were what we should be." Conformed to Christ, especially in the likeness of his crucifixion, Christians receive a new identity that imparts to us extraordinary strength. Through suffering we become what we should be. Suffering inures us to the harms of the world in such a way that we even welcome them with "a great desire to do something for God," in the words of St. Teresa of Avila. This is the heart of Christian sacrifice.

Every affliction endured in this grace-filled spirit becomes redemptive, as Thomas à Kempis observes: "Nothing that is suffered for God's sake, no matter how small, can pass without a reward." As a result, suffering ironically stands as an invaluable source of truest joy. St. Therese of Lisieux testifies that "suffering itself becomes the greatest of joys when one sees it as the most precious of treasures."

How then should we deal with the mystery of suffering? The spiritual masters teach us to approach suffering from within the embrace of God's love. Brother Lawrence of the Resurrection writes: "If we knew how much God loves us we would always be ready to receive from him even the most painful trials." Secondly, the saints counsel us to be mindful of our communion with them in the midst of our sufferings, and to rely on their friendship. In a preeminent way, the Blessed Mother, Our Lady of Sorrows, aids us in our own sorrow. St. Louis de Montfort assures us: "The faithful servants of the Blessed Virgin Mary bear these crosses with greater ease, merit and glory, than others." And thirdly, it is important to keep in mind that it is in the experience of suffering that we personally know authentic peace, joy, and fulfillment. As Brother Lawrence reminds us, "God does not allow a soul entirely devoted to him to have any other pleasures than with him." Suffering serves to keep our devotion to God undivided, wholehearted, and absolute.

Devotion to the Blessed Virgin Mary

The Blessed Virgin Mary holds a privileged place in the faith-lives of the Catholic spiritual masters. They recognize fervent devotion to Mary as an essential and providential way for Christians to deepen their relationship with God. St. Louis de Montfort teaches: "Devotion to Mary is necessary to all people simply to secure their salvation.... I do not believe that any person can achieve intimate union with Our Lord unless he has established a very deep union with the Blessed Virgin and a great dependence on her help."

Our devotion to Mary serves as one of the principal ways that God shares the richness of his life with us. The author of *The Cloud of Unknowing* directs us: "Bind yourself to Jesus in faith and love so that belonging to him you may share all he has and enter the fellowship of those who love him. This is the communion of the blessed and these will be your friends: our Lady, St. Mary, who was full of grace at every moment, and all the blessed in heaven and on earth." Mary is the Lord's priceless gift to us.

By accepting the Blessed Mother as God's gift to us, we attain the humility with which Mary accepted everything in her own life as God's gift. In this sense, Mary is our truest exemplar and model of the Church. Jean-Pierre de Caussade notes: "Filled with joy, Mary regarded everything she had to do or suffer at any moment of her life as a gift from him who showers delights upon those who hunger and thirst only for him." This same spirit inspires Thomas à Kempis to pray before receiving Holy Communion: "O Lord God, I long to receive you this day with such reverence, praise, and honor, with such gratitude, worthiness and love, with such faith, hope, and purity as that with which your most holy Mother, the glorious Virgin Mary, longed for and received you when she humbly and devoutly answered the angel who announced to her the mystery of the Incarnation."

Like the love we share with one another, the devotion we give to Mary should be divinely informed. Julian of Norwich instructs us: "All who delight in God should take delight in Mary, and in the delight that he has in her and she in him." By delighting in Mary the way God delights in her, we come to realize more deeply how much God delights in us and desires our good. That divine desire is expressed in our relationship with the Blessed Mother. St. Francis de Sales counsels us: "With your inward eyes behold the Blessed Virgin who maternally bids you: 'Courage, my child, do not spurn my Son's desires or the many sighs I have cast forth for you as I yearn with him for your eternal salvation.'"

The promise of our salvation is held secure by virtue of our relationship with the Blessed Mother. The Lord pledges to St. Catherine of Siena: "My goodness has decreed that anyone at all, just or sinner, who holds Mary in due reverence will never be snatched or devoured by the infernal demon." A story from *The Little Flowers of St. Francis* verifies this pledge. The Blessed Mother appears at the bedside of a dying, fretful friar and calls him by name, saying: "Do not fear, my son. For I have seen your tears. And I have come to give you a little consolation before you leave this life."

The maternal mediation of Mary is manifold in our life of faith. The Blessed Mother remains instrumental in producing the personal rectitude and conformity to Jesus that makes us saints. As St. John of the Cross teaches: "God moves certain souls to do works that are in harmony with his will and ordinance, and they cannot be moved toward others. Thus the works and prayer of these souls always produce their effect. Such was the prayer and work of our Lady, the most glorious Virgin."

The Lord asks us to be one with the Blessed Mother so that our actions might be as holy and effective as her own. St. Teresa of Avila advises: "Take every opportunity of making the saints your advocates so that they may do battle for you." However, we must remember that the principal battleground lies within ourselves. St. Ignatius of Loyola directs his exercitants to depend on Mary as an instrument of purification in their lives. They are to ask the Blessed Mother to grant them a saving knowledge of sinfulness and worldliness, along with the fervent desire to amend their lives. St. Therese of Lisieux also professes the purifying power of the Blessed Mother: "When I am preparing for Holy Communion, I picture my soul as a piece of land and I beg the Blessed Virgin to remove from it any rubbish that would prevent it from being free."

Brother Lawrence of the Resurrection acknowledges the delight he receives in praying to the Blessed Mother through the Rosary. As we reflect when praying the Hail Mary on the blessedness of Jesus, the fruit of Mary's womb, St. Augustine informs us that we too are required mystically to return to that place of New Life: "Our true life came down to us and suffered our death and slew death out of the abundance of his own life. And he thundered, calling aloud to us to return to him into that secret place from which he came forth to us — coming first into the Virgin's womb, where he espoused the human creation, our mortal flesh, that it might not be forever mortal."